Dear Hugo

A novel by Herbie Sykes

Dear Hugo
© Herbie Sykes, 2022

Herbie Sykes has asserted his right under the Copyright, Designs and Patents Act, 1988, to be identified as the Author of this work. All rights reserved. No part of this publication may be reproduced or transmitted in any form or by any means, electronic or mechanical, including photocopying, recording, or any information storage or retrieval system, without prior permission in writing from the publishers. No responsibility for loss caused to any individual or organisation acting on or refraining from action as a result of the material in this publication can be accepted by Rapha, Rapha Editions, Bluetrain Publishing Ltd. or the author.

Published in 2022 by Rapha Racing Ltd.
Imperial Works,
18 Tileyard,
London,
N7 9AH

Published for Rapha Editions,
in arrangement with Bluetrain Publishing Ltd
bluetrainpublishing.com

Rapha founder: Simon Mottram
Publishing directors: Tom McMullen and Francois Convercey
Publishing co-ordinator: Melissa Richards

Editor: Guy Andrews
Publishing editor: Taz Darling
Art direction: Bluetrain
Images: Linda Duong and Keith George

Book design: Leo Field with Bruna Osthoff

Printed in the UK by Pureprint Group

ISBN 978-1-912164-19-6

All rights reserved

rapha.cc

All images © as page numbers:
Getty: Dust jacket, 19, 25, 26, 34, 51, 55, 65, 75, 76, 79, 88, 96, 112, 128
PresseSports / Offside: Dust jacket, 33, 65
Herbie Sykes Archive: 6, 25, 33, 34, 45, 55, 56, 66
ETH-Bibliothek Zürich, Bildarchiv: Dust jacket, 62, 95, 112
Staatsarchiv Aargau Ringier Bildarchiv: Dust jacket (Walter L. Keller), 5, 26 (Milou Steiner), 20 (Schleiniger), 33, 56 (ATP), 46, 96, 102 (Siegbert Maurer)

Dear Hugo

A novel by Herbie Sykes

Preface

I've talked to (and written about) a lot of old cyclists. I've concluded that they're almost all fantasists, that so am I, and so too most of the people who tell their stories. The good news is that I know much less about cycling now than I did when I started, and I'm pleased to report that the unlearning continues apace. I'm still hopelessly in love with it, but through patience and occasional rigour I've established two basic rules. I apply them assiduously, and they are as follows:

Rule 1) I never trust anything I read about cycling.
Rule 2) I never trust anything I write about cycling.

I therefore assumed, before I started this book, that most of what I thought I knew about Hugo Koblet would be untrue. Certainly it would be wholly inadequate, and irrefutably it would miss the point entirely. It turned out I was right about all of that, and that's why I had to write it as a book of imagined correspondence. You may or may not like it, but be assured it's much better and much more accurate than the biography I'd been minded to produce.

Whilst I'd like to report that it's "based on a true story", the fact is I can't. It's based on a story which is commonly "believed" to be true, but which is half the story at best. For your part, therefore, just assume it's all made up. If – and I admit it's a sizeable if – you get to the end of it, assume that the way it makes you feel is the truth about Hugo Koblet. It's not much, but it's the best I could do.

The book is littered with typing, spelling and syntax errors. Apologies in advance, but I wanted to be faithful to the imaginary letters, and to the imaginary people who wrote them.

Thanks

I'm extremely grateful to Daniel Sprecher and Peter Schnyder for their time and understanding. Thanks to Peter Hugo Koblet, Hugo's nephew, and to both Martin Born and Marc Locatelli, to Fabian Guggenbühl at Vivi Kola, and to Katie Grinstead at Outstanding Eyewear. Also thanks to Jenifer Nicholson, who really does have lovely handwriting, Bruna and Leo who struggled to fit a lifetime of correspondence into this book and to everyone at Rapha and Bluetrain, thanks to all.
Herbie Sykes

8th June 2021

Hello.

It started with this photograph, just in case you were wondering. It taken on 17 August 1947, on the second day of the Tour de Suisse. Most people assume the three of us were together becausse we were in the same place and we were more or less the same age. However i'd never met the other 2 and still today I have no idea who they were. I assume they lived nearby, but maybe not. All I can tell you about them is that they didn't seem to know anything about bike racing. I found that dissappointing at the time because for me it wasn't like that at all. I knew quite a lot about bike racing and I was there because it was important.

I can't go to my grave without explaining everything, but if it's all the same I won't write my name. Technicly what I did was wrong, and I suppose you could even say it was criminal. I've had to live with that for nearly over 50 years but I know, in my heart, that I did it for the right reasons. You can be the judge of that if you want but my conscience is clear.

Anyway my sister says I'VE NOThing much to lose, and I suppose shes right. I'm near the end and they're not likely to throw an 84-yearsold man in prison for something he did when he was in his30s. I just wanted you to know that because I think it's important, you see?. The other thing you should know is that it wasn't something I did litely. I thought about it a lot at the time, and I also thought about what would have happened if I hadn't done it. I decided that would hav have been much worse and thankfully I haven't changed my mind.

I"m doing this while I still have the streangth. If it finishes mme off then so be it butif there's one thing I've learned in this world it's that you have to get things straight. So that's what I'M going to try to do before it's too late! . (Excuse the typing – I haven't used this thing for 40 years and I nevere w as much for words.).

Dear Hugo

9th June 2021

My father was mad on cycling, you see? His favourite was racer was Ferdi Kübler and he talked to me about him a lot. Ferdi had won the firststage at the Tour de France thbat year and my dad had shown me the newspaper article with the photo of him wearing the maillot jaune.

I remember that we were sat at the kitchen table waiting for mum to serve our supper. Dad shouted "YES FERDI YES!" and hugged me quite hard. Mum wasn't happy because he wasn't supposed to read his newspaper at the table. He was supposed to read it after when me and my sistser were in bed. My mum would listen to music or something on the wireless and he would smoke his cigarette and read the news. Anyway that particcular day it wsn't like that and that was probably because the Tour de France was such a big thing forhim. Mum went " PuT THAT PAPER AWAY AND STOP LEARNING HIM BAD HABITS!"My dad winked at me and I winked back. We had a sort of secret code where things like that were concerned, and my mum and sister didn't know about it.

I used to cut the photos of the famous riders out. I'd stick them in my scrap book and write profeils of the riders and reports of what happened in the races. I knew all the Swiss riderd and I knew about the big racesin France,Belgium, Italay and Switzerland. I'd looked them all up at the library and I always read dad's paper the following day when I got home from school (He'd finished with it you see, so it was always waiting for me when I got in.) I used to read it before he got back from work and that was when I used to cut out the interesting bits for my scrap book. Usually I'd show him what I'd cut out and he would make suggestierns. Then afterwards I'd do the scrap book while my sister read her book or organized her things or whatever before we turned the lamp out. So that's how I became interssted in bike racing you see?

10th June 2021

When the photo was taken it was the first week in AUGUST because the Tour de Suisse was afetr the Tour that year and not before it. I knew the race was goingto be starting in Zurich because I'd seen in the paper and there was going be a big parade on the Friday evening to present the riders. My dad asked me if I wanted to go and I said I did. He said that was settled then so I went to the foundry where he worked and met him when he came out at 4.30. We took the tram to the observatry, and it only too about ten minutes.

   There was a big car park there (it's gone now9), and it was full of proppagandar cars and trucks. They were mainly ordinary cars and trucks with loudhailers on them but some of them were really spectaculer. I remember one had a giant tin of meat on it, and one looked like something from outer space. One had a pair of big, smiling red lips on the radiator grille, and there were others that had toothpaste tubes, giant clocks,huge beer-bottles and all sorts. There were smiling people going round the crowd giving things away for people to try :– free samples I suppose you would call them. One of the trucks had a musical group playing music and there was a woman singing. IT WSas popular music from the mountains and a few people were singing along and clapping. Tthere was a drunk guy who kept falling over and getting back up, and a police-man was watching hm. I was watching the police-man because he didn't seeme sure what to do. The drunk man wasn't any harm but you shouldn't make a show of youself like tbhat in public. I hadn't known anything like this before and I got a load of souvenirs. I got some Ovomaltine ,a pencil and some leaflets. A clown who was on stilts came up and gave me a slice of cheese from holland and a swiss little Swiss flag on a stick.
I think there were some mints as well. Dda bought me an ice-cream but he made me prmise not to say anything to mum about that.

   After about half an hour looking round and getting things we went to the front and waited for the riders to be shown. Dad had newspaper and he talked me through the names of all the riders one by one. I was looking forward to seeing Coppi and Bartali, and dad reckoned that if Kübler didn't wwin then Bartali probably would. He said he was the best climber but I wasn't sure about that because Coppi had beaten him at the Giro and a Belgian fellow had beaten him at the Romandie's Tour. I'd decided I was going to side with Bartali though. The reason was that it was only right because he was my dads favrite and he'd been the one who'd inrtroduced me to cycling in the first place. Besides, they called Bartali "THE Iron man" and I thought that was great. ~~A Lot~~

Dear Hugo

13th June 2021

Some of the riders looked small and quite funny. What I mean is that I hadnever seen them before and I wasn't used to them like that so I expected them all to be big and powerful like in the photos. (Not Robic and Schär because I knew they were short-arses.). Buchwalder was a bit scary because his teeth were missing and he looked like he was from mediaeval times. One of the Italians had a beard and he said he wouldn't shave until he won a stage. The people around us laughed, and dad said he'd need to be careful because he had no chance of winning a stage and it wasn't easy to ride a bike if you had a beard down to the floor. I knew about OCKErs (Stan) and I already liked him a lot. He was small and he was always smiling even if he came second a lot and so it seemed to nme that he was a very nice person. There was Mahe from France, Diederich from Luxemburg and an English rider I can't remember. Dad told me to forget about the Englisher because he probably wouldn't last long in the race. Hesaid it would be too hard for him because he was probably more used to playing tennis and drinking tea on his lawn. I aksked him what that meant but he didnot have time toanswer because suddenly he went "Look – There's Leo!". It was Mr Amberg from the bike shop near ourhhouse. I often saw him riding and d ad was his friend. The announcer chap asked him some questions, and some of the crowd clapped and chaerred when he left.

    Other riders came and went but it got much more craowded around us. More and more people started showing up because they'd finished work and they wanted to see the champions, you see?. Dad was talking to the bloke next to him and that was when I lost my place at the front. After that I could only really see the cyclist's legs most of the time. If I craned my neck or stood on tip- toes I'd get a glimpse of their heads and bodies, and I definitely saw Croci-Torti, Diggelmann and Knecht. It was quite tiring being on tip- toes but I desperately wanted to see Bartali and Kübler and I didn't want to give up..

    I tried not to be upset, and to think about a tactic to see the champions when they came. The one I decided on was to stay on tiptoes for 4 seconds when Coppi came, 8 for Bartali and 12 for Kübler. I knew it would be hard, staying on tip toes like that, but I was good at gymnastics and I was used to doing that sorrt of thing with my sister. I knew that I could do at least 10 seconds and that my mum would be impressed if I managed 12.

I needn't have worried because when Coppi came dad turned round to me and said, "lok - there's Fausto!" He lifted me up and put on his shoulders and at first I didn'yt know what to think and I felt a bit stupid. As I saw it I was was too big to be on his shoulders! and the bloke behind us started complainnning. Dad told him to shut up, and so did the bloke he'd been speaking with. He said, "he's only a kid" but as far as I was concerned I'd stopped being a kid when I'd started middle school. Anyway it was worth it because after a while I wasn't embarressed any more and I had the best view of all when BARTali came. I remember everyone gasped because he'd won the Tour and the Giro and they said he was the greatest climber of all time.. When Kübler came my dad started shouting and waving, so I did as dwell. The problem was that inmy excitement I dropped my cheese. I was holding it in the same hand as my flag, and I suppose i must have waved it too hard.I remember thinking it was a shame because I'd wanted to give my sister that cheese.

On the tram home my dad said he had a plan. Iasked him what I was and he said I had to wait and see. We home about 8 and he asked mum if she wanted to go to see her sister on sunday and maybe have a picnick.Mum said that would be great and dad said 2 "that's settled then. We can get the train to Thusis, and then get the bus to see Ilke and Bernhard. after lunch we'll go for a walk and have a picnic." My auntie Ilke and my mum always made big tasty plum cakes when we went and my sister and I always played with the rabbits. That left my ddad the uncle and they just talked and smoked while my uncle showed my dad what he'd been making. He was always doing things with wires and metal you see? He made radios and airoplanes and all sorts. He made a bomb once andmade it explode in the lake.

When I went to bed I asked dad what the plan was again buit he wasn't telling. He just said "just you wait and see matey".

....

15th June 2021

On Sunday morning we all were up early and we walked to the station. When we got there Dad bought a 'paper from the kiosk and then we caught the train. I remember it was already quite hot so we were all looking forward to getting out of Zurich and being in the hills. At first we had the carriage to ourselves but tyhen a soldier got one and sat

Dear Hugo

next to my sister. The problem was you could smell alcohol on his breath and my mum wasn't having that. She told him to move because it wasnt right that me and my sister would have to be near him. I ccould tell that my dad was embarressed but the soldier he apologized to us and just got up and left without arguing.My mum was like that you see? My dad would never have done something like that because he hated arguements. You see my father was quite a shy person.After a while dad nudged me and winked. He went "watcth this!", but only under his breath. That meant that I could see what he was saying but my mum and sister couldn't hear it. He picked up the newspaper and went to the sports pages first. Aftger a couple of minutes he went,, "oh look! the bike race is passing right by Ilke's village! Maybe we'll see the riders while we have our picnic!" Mum looked at me and said, "well what a coibncidence! who'd have thought it?" and my dad winked at me. That had been the plan all along, you see? My mum wasn't bothered because she was looking forward to seeing auntie Ilke and my sister wasn't bothered so she just carried on colouring in. Mym um was just ptretending to be surprised but I don't think she was. She was happy really because she knew me and mty dad liked cycling.

 You have to understand that for mew this was a very big thing. What I mean is that I hadn't seen any actual racing before and now we were going to the mountains to see Bartali, KüBLER AND Coppi. Dda showed me the paper and it said that Bartali already had the jersey. There'd been three stages the previous day. The last one had finished in Davos and they'd gone over the Wolfgang Pass. It said Bartali had attacked and dropped all theothers. Dad told me that if we went quite high we'd get a good view of them.. He said it would be best if we went to Zillis, or somewhere like that, because that way the champions would already have dropped the others. He told my mum the mountains were alwaysthe best place to watch cycling and she nodded and carried on combing mu sister's hair. Dad winked attt me and I winked back in our code.

 We went to my aunt's house and after lunch the rabbits and some radio we set off on foot. Me, my uncle Bernhard and my dad were together, and when I looked behind I could see my mum, auntie and sister. They were nattering and giggling and I remember thinking my mum looked reaklly happy and really beautiful in her dress. It wasn't too steep so I was able to keep up quite easily . As we were walking along the road all the proppagandar cars came flying by. I got a paper hat, a bib with a cow on it and some leaflets (when I got home ip ut them in my scrap book.) When the females arrived we drank lemonade and ate more plum cake. Mum told me to calm down because I was too agitated. Dadsaid "Let him be won't you? of course he's agitated – it's his 1st time at a race!."

   I just remembered that one of the cars had a big hailer on top and there was atalking guy in it. His job was to tell you what was happening in the race and he went something like "So young Koblet is perssisting with his attack. He has a minute on a group containing Kübler, Coppi, Bartali and Bresci"

   I didn't catch anything else because the car was going quite fast, but my dad told us Koblet was from the bakery in Ausser-sihl. He said he'd seen him training at the outdoor track at Oerlikon and he was tall for a bike rider. He said he had blond hair and we'd see that he was very styleish on the bike. He had in America doing Six Day races in USA and he'd done well there. Amberg had been looking after him and it was his first big proper road race. Dad said we'd stopped and bought gingerbread at that bakery once, on the way back from my gran's house. I remember saying, "so I suppose in that case we can say we know Koblet then?" and my dad said that he supposed we did. II thought that was great so i made a mental note to tell everyone that Koblet was a friend of mine and I used to visit him in his bakery. Then the motorbikes came and dad said thee riders would be alomg any second so we'd best be getting ready.

   We had our spot but just as I was getting ready those other two boys appeared (that's what you can see in the photograph=). I don't know why I started running but I know that I ran for ages trying to keep up with Koblet. They ran as well, but not for as long as I did. . It was as if some of the energy from Koblet's body was was transfered into me. my body). I was looking at him as I ran alongside him and he looked at me for a second and smiled. That bgave me even more energy and even more speed, so that's probably why I couldn't stop running and afterwards I couldn't calm down.

Dear Hugo

16th June 2021

I saw the other riders but I can't say much about them. Bartali came past with Bresci who was another little one and and then Kübler came with Ockers and Depredhomme. Coppi came with some others but he was talking and he just seemed to float by. I wasn't really able to concentrate anyway because by then the pow er was running out and I didn't have energy left. I t was probably jusst all a bit of a daze. The only thing I remember clearly was that nighht when I was in bed because dad came to say good night and he didn't normally do that because mum did it. He said "So what do you think then matey?" I told him it had been the best day of my life, and asked if we could go back to the bakery in Aussersihl to see Koblet. He said, "we'll see. Goodnight champ". (He often called me Champ)

    The thing to keep in mind is that I STILL THink it was the best day of my life even if it happened 74 years ago. It was the day I properly discovered cycling and the day I met Hugo Koblet. it's also the reason I did what I did so even if you won't necessarily agree with it you might at least have an understanding of it .

It is time for me to go now. Though we won't be together anymore, I want you to know that I love you both very much. Perhaps I have not been father that you deserved, but never forget that I tried to be the best I could. I hope that, one day, you will be able to understand me & to forgive me.

Goodbye, beautiful boys.

Father.

Aussersihl Primary School, Kernstrasse 45, 8004, Zurich. Tel: 77.145
Head teacher: Peter Klodt

....

Term report:		June 1935
Student:		Hugo Koblet (21-5-25)
Year:		5
Form teacher:		Mr. F. Hermann

....

Writing:	4/6.	Hugo writes nicely, and has no difficulty with new concepts. Calligraphy above average for a boy.
Reading:	6/6.	Hugo is a very fluent reader.
Mathematics:	3/6.	Not particularly interested. Loses concentration on occasion.
Geography:	6/6.	Has a fascination for different places and cultures. Particularly enthusiastic about the Americas.
Languages:	6/6.	Has a natural aptitude for languages, and is keen to learn.
Religious Education:	3/6.	Average.
Gymnastics:	6/6.	Excellent. Though Hugo is very slender, his natural athleticism belies his fragile appearance.
Art:	4/6.	Above average.
Behaviour	6/6	

....

Notes: Hugo is unfailingly polite and good-natured, and this makes him popular with his classmates. He is highly intelligent and eager to please at all times. Everyone appreciates the cakes he brings in to school and I'm pleased to report that, notwithstanding the situation, his behaviour remains impeccable. He is a joy to be around.

10.05.43
LEO AMBERG
BIKES & MOPEDS
Swiss champion;
1937, 1938
2x Tour de France
stage winner 1937
Giro d'Italia
stage winner 1938

HUGO,

I SAW YOU RACE AND I think you can become a GOOD rider. Diggelmann agrees.

   you need to leave the lighting factory AND THIS IS because The fumes FROM THE FORGE will damage your LUNGS. YOU CAN help me instead HRE WORKING. You are too skinny. we will start with your chest because IT NEEDS building up. I will arrange a decent track bike because you'll have to stop with the road for a WHILE, it's for the best,

   You will train in the mornings before the shop opens, WE start at 6 sharp, In the evenings you can train at THE TRACK. do as diggelmann says AND DON'T EVER BE LATE. Discipline is everything IN CYCLING.

Amberg

6.10.44

DIPLOMA
Awarded to: Hugo Koblet
Swiss Amateur Champion, Individual Pursuit Oerlikon Velodrome

5.05.46
LEO AMBERG
BIKES & MOPEDS
Swiss champion;
1937, 1938
2x Tour de France
stage winner 1937
Giro d'Italia
stage winner 1938

Dear h,

WELL I told you I'd make a professional cyclist of you! Good luck, dear boy!, don't try to cut corners, RIDE WITH YOUR HEAD, AND remember what I told you ABOUT THE DESCENTS!

l

```
11.11.49
Gino Bartali
Via Chintigiana 177
Ponte a Ema
Firenze

Hugo Koblet
Hildastrasse 3
Zurich, Swiss
```

Dear Koblet I am decided that i don't need you next season. I remember the stage you won at Romandie. You were bravo but i also remember that we of the classiffication group let you go that day . with the crashes and injuries you haven't ridden since so i have no way of knowing if you're fully recuperated ? for all i know you might be kaput and i don't know if you can ride for three weeks which is what I need so what am i supposed to do ? It's true you have potentiality but also lots of Italian riders are like that therefore for me its better that way because you maybe can't so for the bikes what use is it ? if i was you i would concentrate on pursuiting and the Sixes . You seem to be a good one on the track so maybe focus on that why not ?

Good luck anyhow from Bartali.

```
Hochtstrasse 9                                    BY HAND
Schaffenhaausen

Dear Hugo,

I've been thinking about our "situation" a lot and
I've concluded it's not  going to work. You seem to
have a problem with commitment - except where your
mother iS concerned - and eviddently we want totally
different things.
I don't think it's unreasonable that I want a
settled, "normal" life. With the cycling, though,
I never know whether I'm coming or going. When you
were in America doing that Six-Day race with
Diggelmann, I didn't like it one little bit. I didn't
know where you were or who you were with, and after
what happened with that Angela (or Angelika?) girl my
head was spinning just thinking about it all. Now you
say you're going back to America, and goodness knows
what will happen. Maybe you'll find a girl who's happy
to watch you racing your bike for hours, and then sit
around listening to you talk to your mother...
You say everything is fine, but you have what my
mother calls "the roving eye". I see it when we're
out together,  and my friends have noticed it too. →
```

Le grand prix de l'hôtel de Fribourg, 4th June 1944. Junioren (116 km): 1. Charles Guyot (Lausanne) 2. Hans Roth (Zürich) 3. Hugo Koblet (Zürich) 4. René Jeannin (Genf) 5. Marcel Maire (La Chaux-de-Fonds) 6. M Cozzi (Genf) alle gleiche Zeit

Championats Suisses sur route 2nd July 1944 Junioren (139.3 km): 1. Hugo Koblet (Dietikon) 3:58:50 2. Werner Röhrling (Zürich) 3. Paul Baumann (im Felde) 4. G. Hülimann (Zug) 5. Willi Briner (Zürich) 6. Werner Schönenberger (Seebach).

Championats Suisses sur piste à Zurich, 10th May 1945, Poursuite amateurs, 4km – Classement Finale: 1. Hugo Koblet (Zurich) 5' 14" 2. Jean-Pierre Burtin (Genève) 3. Stéphan Peterhans (Fislibach)

Réunion internationale à Oérlikon velodrome, 4th August 1946 Poursuite Professionnel: 1. Hugo Koblet (Suisse) 6'34"2 pour 5km, soit nouveau record de la piste d'Oerlikon! 2. Blanchet (France) 6'37"2.

You cyclists sure have Stamina!! Can we do it again tonite?

→ Brigitte says you're just not capable of being
faithfull and I hate it that I don't trust you.
I love you, but you don't make me happy and your mum
is always fussing around. I understand that you don't
have a father but you can't fill his shoes and you
certainly can't be the man he never was. That's not
normal Hugo, and it's not normal that I feel as if
I'm the one intruding.
I'm sorry but it's all just a bit too much, so I'm
going to England after all. My heart is broken, and
I'm telling you this way because it's best we don't
see each other in the meantime. So this is goodbye,
dear Hugo. Good luck with your cycling career, and
regards to your mother and to poor Dölf.

Ruthli.

07.04.50
Cicli Guerra
Via Giulio Ferreri
20153 Milano
Tel: 3929

Hugo Koblet
Hilda strassse 3
8004
Zurich
Switzerland

Dear Koblet,
Nice it was to meet you at Lakke Lugano. My friend Zanazzi
says he have raced you in 1946 and he could see you were
a very good one. Zanazzi knows everything and you have
much possibbility. So i can say you are chosen for Giro
d'Italia. It will start in Milan and finishing in Rome (the
winner will meet the Pope because it's a special year. There
are no xxx time trials which is bad foir you. We will be
in Switzerland on stage six and I expect a good there from
you performance. Dupont will ride for the classification
and you will be to fetch bottles for him if he goes good. He
might not and if he doesn't go forward we can decide. We'll
see. Our team will be like this:
Dupont (BEL)
Cerami (BEL-ITA)
Bizzi (ITA)
Marini (ITA
Koblet (SWI)
Weilenmann L (SWI)
Weilebmann G (SWI)
We'll see each othera at Milan-Vicenza on 25April to
concretize the things.
Best wishes,
Learco Guerra

Dear Hugo

```
23.05.50                                           BY HAND
Our little house

My dearest, most handsome Hugi!

Well you have gone off to the Giro now for the big
adventure you always dreamed of. You always said you
would make it one day, and your brother and I we are
so proud! I hope this letter comes to your hands after
the first stage and that everything has gone goodly!

I am writing because however things happen I will be
your best  most loyal supporter! I remember the
greatest smile on your head when you came home from
your first bicycling! I hope to can see the same smile
on 20 June (or whenever). You are racing against Coppi
and Bartali  but you are best as them and there are no
love things with girls to distract you now.  Stay away
from the girls and trouble to make that everything
will be a success! For  sure something goodly will
happen! You were the stronger at Romandie and everyone
knows you would have been winning without the
puncturing! Please, try not to crash and try to watch
the way Kübler reacts! I know he belongs to another
team but he knows how to do everything. You Swiss boys
must stick together! You will always be my champion!
When you come home I will be waiting with the better
cherry strudel of all times!

With love,
Your devoted mother!

P.S. Yesterday I have went and baught lovely wool!
I started knitting new gloves for my Hugi to bring
them to the hotel in Locarno on 29 May! They will be
the special prize if you can win the stage and will
also be goodly when you reach the cold mountains!
```

```
                                    MODULE 30, 1950 TELEGRAM OFFICE
                                      ISSUED: Antwerp Central, Belgium.
                      DEST: KOBLET CAROVAN GIRO D'ITALIA BOLZANO ITALY
                                             NR079763. 2 JUNE 1950. 11.30
                                                              Words: 34
```

HAD MAGLIA ROSA 3 DAYS 1933. DON'T EAT FOOD FROM HOTEL KITCHEN. ALWAYS SLEEP IN DIFFERENT ROOM. DON'T TAKE FOOD/DRINK FROM FANS. WATCH BIKE DAY+NIGHT. ITALIANS=CHEATS=will DO ANYTHING. STOP. DEMUYSERE

```
                                         MODULE 9/12886 1950 XVI
                                                   TELEGRAM OFFICE
                                       DESTINATION: CAMPOBASSO, ITALY
                                       ISSUED BY: grosse/Zurich dist.9
                                        KOBLET GIRO DITALIA CAMPOBASSO
                                            277 ZURICH-TORINO SD90832.
                                            11 JUNE  1950. 17.25 W 23
```

TWO STAGES LEFT MY WONDERFUL HUGI STREET PINK shop pink all pink COMING TO ROME new dress WE MEET POPE deepest joy MOTHER

Bergstrasse 716,
Uetikon

Hugo Koblet
Zurich

Dear Hugo, ♥♥♥

I wanted to write to you because we met at the parade the day you came home from the Giro! I know there were lots of other girls there, but I hope you remember me all the same. I think you will, because I was the blonde one wearing a pink silk scarf and pink lipstick. You said, "Pink - like my maglia rosa!" Then you signed my card, and for a moment I was such light-headed that I thought I might faint!

I forgot to tell you that my name is MARTINA and I'm from Uetikon. I listened to the Giro on the radio with my

Dear Hugo

dad. He loves cycling but he doesn't know how I personally feel about you because it's a secret thing and personal between us. My brother said I'd make a fool of myself by writing to you but he's just being foolish and I don't care what he thinks. I will be 18 soon so I think I'm old enough to decide for myself thank you very much! ♥ I like music, dancing and having fun. I can sew, and I can speak French quite good and Italian not so good. I'm teaching to myself English as well. I listen to music on the wireless and write down the words they sing. Sometimes I get confused and the words don't have sense. They come out strange and difficult to understand! My mother says I'm good at making cakes and that if I keep improving I will make a good wife. Who knows – maybe one day my dream will come true and I could marry a handsome, famous cyclist from Zurich???

I have enclosed a stamped addressed envelope, so maybe you could write a letter to me and even ask me if we can meet some place in secret! I've also included something else but please don't tell anyone about that!

♥ ♥ ♥

Martina Wagner

15.06.50

Chancellor's Office,
Federal Place,
Bundesplatz 3,
3005-Bern

Hugo Koblet
Hildastrasse 3
8004
Zurich

Dear Mr. Koblet,

It is my very great honour to write to you on behalf of the Swiss Federation, and Swiss people everywhere.

I want to offer my congratulations on your accomplishments in Italy. You'll be aware that you are the first Swiss to win one of the "grand tours", and your "pink jersey" bestows great pride and honour on all of our people. I have heard excellent reports about the way you and your colleagues conducted yourself over there, and for that I offer my heartfelt thanks.

Yours sincerely,

Rt. Hon. Oskar Leichner
Federal Chancellor

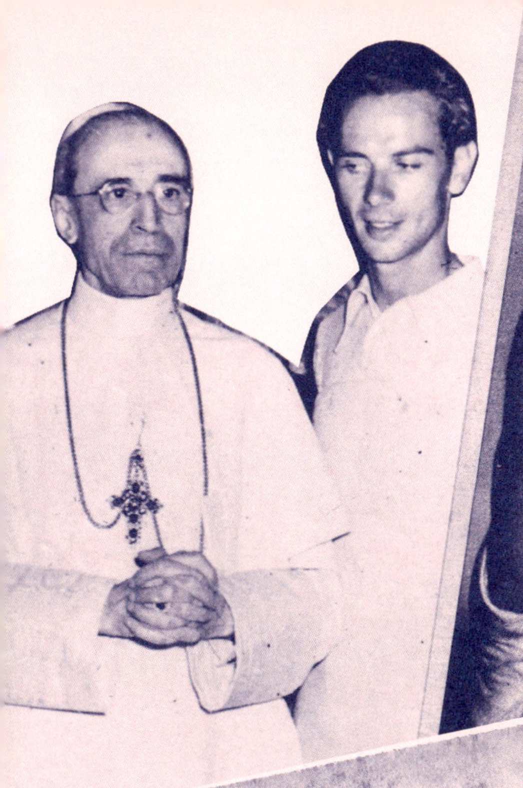

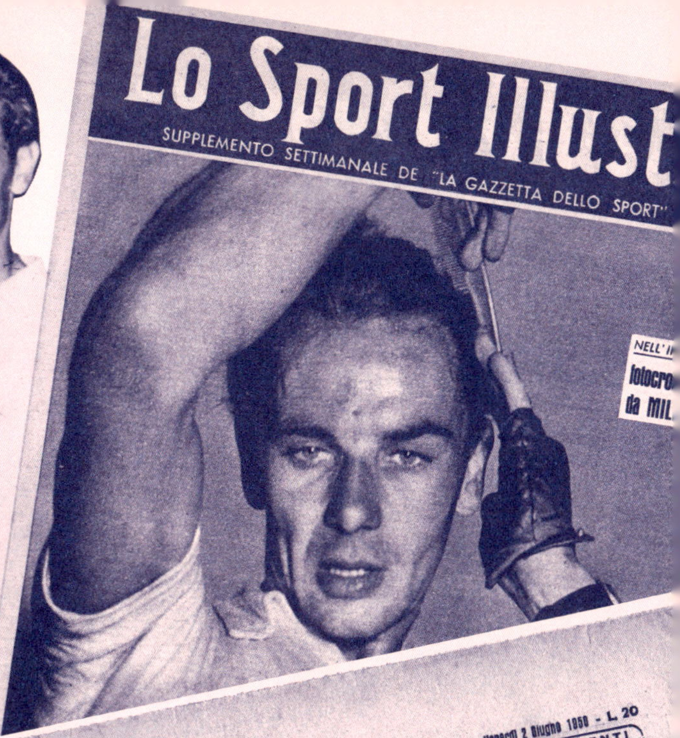

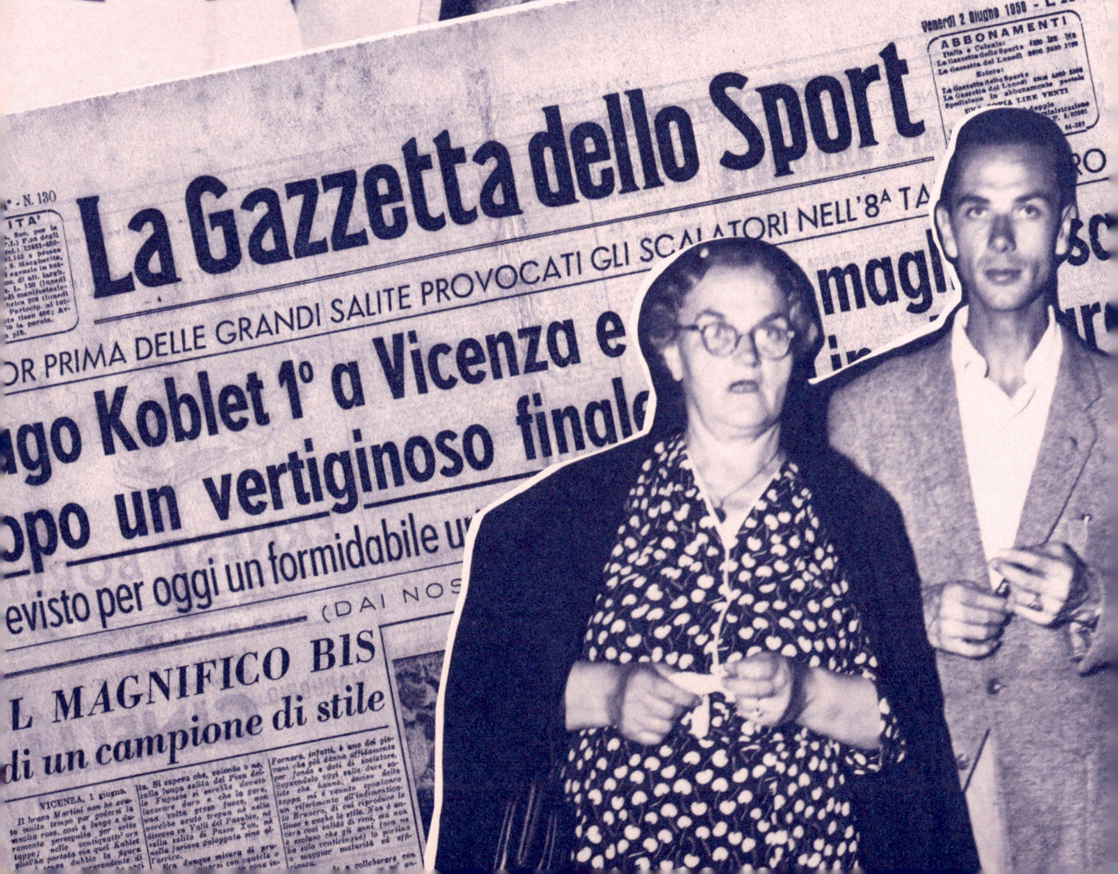

Venerdì 2 Giugno 1950 - L. 20

ABBONAMENTI

N. 130

La Gazzetta dello Sport

PROVOCATI GLI SCALATORI NELL'8a TA

OR PRIMA DELLE GRANDI SALITE

ago Koblet 1° a Vicenza e

opo un vertiginoso final

evisto per oggi un formidabile u

(DAI NOS

L MAGNIFICO BIS

di un campione di stile

VICENZA, 1 giugno.

Il bravo Martini non ha avuto molto tempo per godersi la maglia rosa, così a lungo e duramente perseguita per sette tappe; nelle ventiquattr'ore gliel'ha portata via quel Koblet senza dubbio la figura

la. Si sapeva che, volendo o no, sulla lunga salita del Pian delle Fugazze si sarebbe dovuto lavorare duro e che la gara, una volta preso fuoco, non avrebbe avuto tregua nè nella discesa su Valli del Pasubio, nè sulla salita di Passo Xon, nè nella furiosa galoppata sino all'arrivo.

Era dunque misura di prudenza

Fornara, infatti, è uno dei giovani che più danno affidamento per fondo e doti di scalatore. Seguendolo oggi sulle dure salite che hanno deciso della tappa mi è venuto spontaneo un riferimento all'indimenticato Brunero, di cui riproduce le linee e anche lo stile. Non è ancora così solido di reni, ma non è escluso che gli anni (ora ne ha solo venticinque) lo portino a maggior maturità ed efficienza.

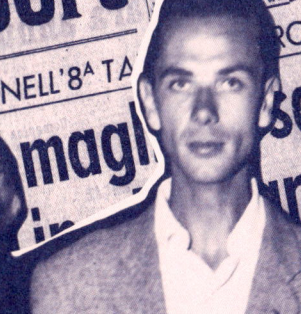

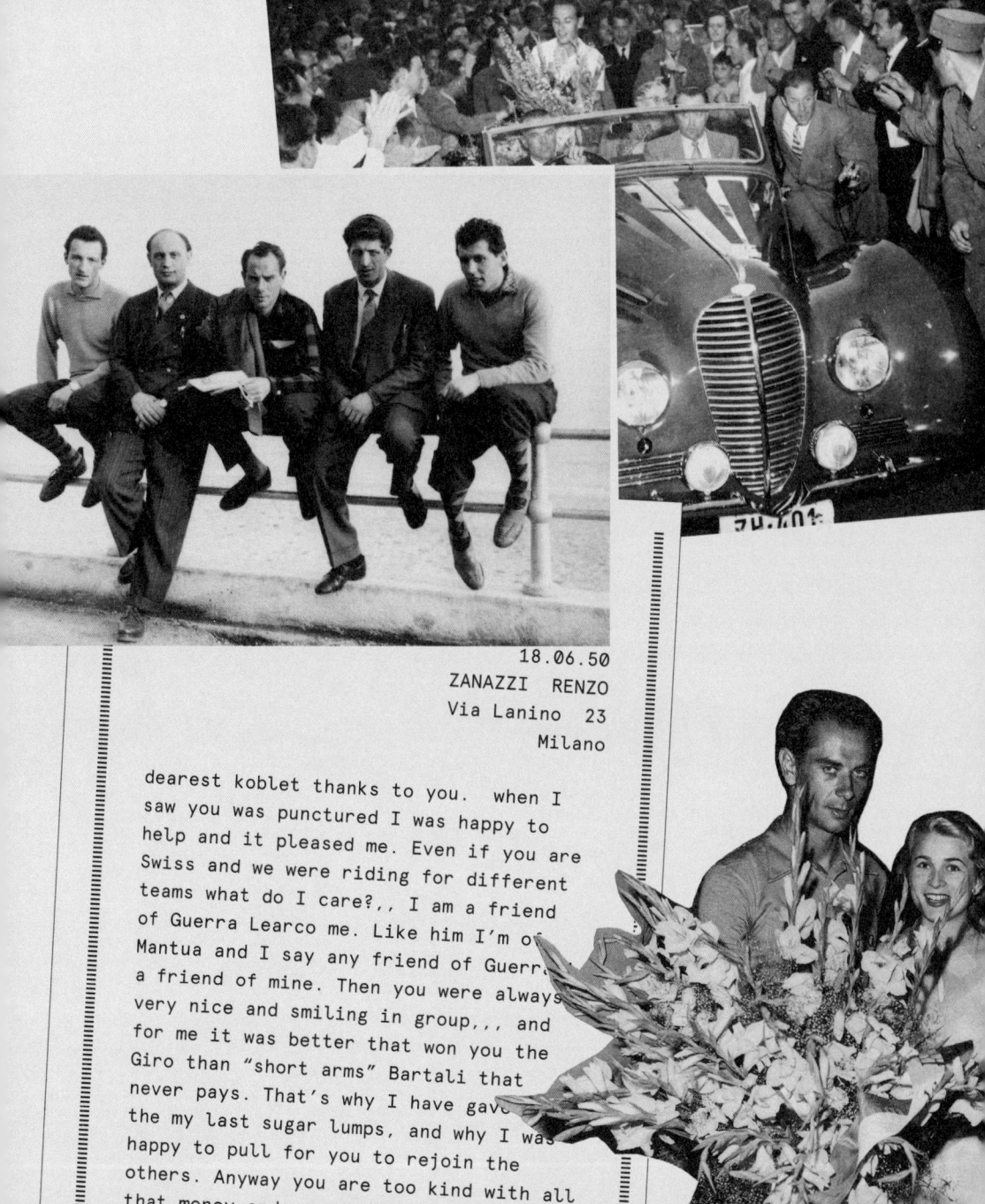

18.06.50
ZANAZZI RENZO
Via Lanino 23
Milano

dearest koblet thanks to you. when I
saw you was punctured I was happy to
help and it pleased me. Even if you are
Swiss and we were riding for different
teams what do I care?,, I am a friend
of Guerra Learco me. Like him I'm of
Mantua and I say any friend of Guerra
a friend of mine. Then you were always
very nice and smiling in group,,, and
for me it was better that won you the
Giro than "short arms" Bartali that
never pays. That's why I have gave
the my last sugar lumps, and why I was
happy to pull for you to rejoin the
others. Anyway you are too kind with all
that money and we are I can say friends.

Zanazzi Renzo

```
16.06.50
La Gazzetta dei
Sportivi
Via Galileo Galilei
7, Milan

Hugo Koblet
Hildastrasse 3
8004
Zurich
```

Dear Koblet,

I write, as is customary, to congratulate you on your victory at the Giro.

This Giro, however, was very different. No non-Italian had ever won before and so, initially at least, it was difficult to accept that a "foreigner" would export our scared pink jersey. It won't have escaped your attention that there was hostility in some quarters when you first captured it. I want to apologise to you for that in the first instance, and to try to offer an explanation in the second.

It's an oft-repeated mantra that "sport has no borders", but it was natural that Italian fans wanted Bartali in pink. He and Coppi are popular here, and following Fausto's crash most people assumed that Gino would win. It goes without saying that he is profoundly catholic. He's also known as the "timeless one", and it's 14 years since he won his first Giro. The idea that he would have an audience with the pope in the autumn of his career was very appealing, and when millions want the same thing and one person – you - stands between them and their dream, it's no surprise that the more extreme elements would wish you ill.

Fortunately the initial hostility evaporated over the course of the final week. That was extraordinary, and that, dear Koblet, was a direct consequence of your human qualities and your behaviours. Your character, elegance and your innate dignity won over the Italian public, and for that we owe you a debt of gratitude. Few expected you to win the Giro, but that doesn't alter the fact that you were the consummate maglia rosa. In fact I would go so far as to say that you were precisely the maglia rosa that the race needed at this time.

A final thought on the racing itself. Cycling is synonymous with sufferance. Its leitmotifs are endurance, perseverance and intense discomfort. In you I saw something completely different, something I'd not witnessed in the previous 32 editions of the Giro. Whilst the others battled over the Dolomites, you floated between them. I saw Girardengo and Binda, and latterly Bartali and Coppi. What I hadn't seen, at least until now, was a champion so sublimely graceful on a racing bicycle. We look forward to welcoming you back next year.
Emiliano Colombini

Dear Hugo

```
                              TELEGRAM CERT. 1950 XVI
                                   POST OFFICE TRENTO
      DESTINATION: THE CYCLIST KOBLET, Zurich, SWITZLAND
                              ISSUED BY: tRENTINO ii/b
                                              WORDS: 28
           02TRENTO-CENTRALINEA MILANO-ZURICH TAA06/MI11956.
                              DATE/TIME: 17 JUNE  1950. 10.32
                                                    l.5 w.29
```

CONGRATULATIONS - A true CHAMPION! Convolescing IN TRENTO. COOL AIR/PEACE. PELVIS PAINFUL (3 FRACTURES) BUT WILL HEAL. SHAME we COULDN'T RACE together – mAY BE next year. COPPI.

26.06.50

Obergass 3,
Eglisau. Tel: 841

Hugo Koblet
Hildastrasse 3
8004
Zurich

Dear Mr Koblet,

First I'd like to congratulate you on your Tour de Suisse. I have been a keen cycling fan all my life but I've never seen a performance like yours on the stage to Bellinzona. I suppose we ought to have expected something miraculous, but what you did was worthy of Coppi.

　　It's a shame we won't see you at the Tour, but hopefully Kübler and the boys will give us something to cheer about. With Coppi absent the race looks wide open.

　　As you will have noticed, we are sponsoring the Swiss races now. As we see cycling as a healthy pastime for young people, we're keen for our product to be associated with it as much as possible. We want for Vivi Kola to be synonymous, and we're developing an idea to market it as "the cyclist's beer".

　　With that in mind, I'm interested in meeting with you personally. I'd like to discuss a sponsorship arrangement which will effectively make you an ambassador for our brand. My belief is that it could be beneficial to us and lucrative for you, and to that end I've set some time aside for next Monday morning, 11 July. If that's not possible please let me know, but otherwise I look forward to seeing you here at 10 o'clock.

Yours sincerely,
Emile Reinle

```
29.06.50
G. BRAEILING S.A.
SOCIÉTE ANONYME
LES CHAUX-FONDS
(SUISSE)

Hugo Koblet
Hildastrasse 3
8004
Zurich
```

Dear Mr Koblet,

As official timekeepers of the cycling union, we welcome opportunities to explore personal sponsorship agreements with the great champions. We already have one in place with Fautso Coppi, and we're keen to discuss a partnership with you.

Please, call me on (32) 925.99 at your earliest convenience, or reply by return of post.

Yours sincerely,

Guillaume Braeiling.

```
05.09.50
RENK BROS.
Cars for the Stars
Edelweissstrasse
8048, Zurich. Tel:
97 19 44

Hugo Koblet
Hildastrasse 3
8004
Zurich
```

Dear Koblet,

As you've probably heard, Alfa Romeo clinched the Formula One Championship in Monza on Sunday. It was a wonderful race, and Nino Farina is a worthy champion! Alfa have dominated the series, and the Swiss Grand Prix in particular was a great success. The crowds were large, and of course our "Three Fs" occupied all three podium places.
 Fangio, Farina and Fagioli are wonderful drivers, and now everyone is talking about the "K&K" of Swiss cycling! With your Giro and Kübler's Tour de France, this really is the most wonderful time for our country and her sports fans!
 Alfa Romeo is launching the new 6C 2500SS Supergioiello model into the Swiss market. It's a fantastic car for the more discerning motorist, and as Zurich's premier distributor we'd like to make one available to you (and also to Ferdi) on extended loan.
We will arrange insurance and maintenance, and we'll also provide a generous monthly fuel allowance. You need simply visit the "showroom" and collect the keys. We expect the first cars to arrive in about six weeks, and if you're in agreement I will contact you again then to confirm the arrangements.

Yours sincerely,
Dirk Renk
Managing Director.

Dear Hugo

12 09.50
Engelhartgasse 6
Hietzing 1130
Vienna
Tel: 2162

Hugo Koblet
Hildastrasse 3
Zurich
Switzerland

Dear Hugo,

It was nice to be guest of honour at the race, and also to finally make your acquaintance. I'd heard so much about you beforehand, but I didn't expect to be so… charmed.

    They invited me there to hand out the prizes, so you'll forgive me if I seemed a little overcome when you gave me the flowers. I wasn't expecting to be presented with such a beautiful bouquet, and still less so to ride a lap of honour on your handlebars.

    You asked me to write and tell you all about my new film, and it's very exciting. It's called "Dancing Happy" and it's a romance. We'll begin the shoot in Berlin, but next month we'll do the outdoors scenes at Lake Constance. We will probably be there until Christmas, and we'll stay in Bregenz. Hey - perhaps you could come and be my guest on the set? When I told the guys I'd met you they were very excited, and the sound engineer in particular never stop talking about cycling. I've become quite an expert, and everyone here is DYING to meet you. Sepp, the set designer, asked me to ask you why you comb your hair before being interviewed. I assume it's just because it's good manners to be presentable, especially after such a big effort on the bike. Anyway I told him I'll arrange for you to tell him personally, so you have no choice! You'll be my special guest, and I'll arrange a room for you in a beautiful hotel by the lake.

Write back and let me know when you can come!

With kindest regards,
W

22.09.50
RENK BROS.
Cars for the Stars
Edelweissstrasse
8048, Zurich. Tel:
97 19 44

Hugo Koblet
Hildastrasse 3
8004
Zurich

Dear Hugo,

It was a pleasure to finally meet you the other day, and of course the staff were thrilled too! What most pleased us was the fact that you remain the same smiling "sunny boy", even though you're a big star now.

Italy assures me we'll have the car before 9 November. You'll be able to drive it to Hannover, and hopefully it will bring you luck! I forgot to ask - will you do the Six Day with Diggelmann or with Armin Von Büren?

Re: your preference to receive your vehicle before Kübler, it's no problem! I'll confirm the date anon.

Best,
Renk

```
                                    MODULE 9/12886 1950 XVI
                                    TELEGRAM OFFICE bregenz
                                    d949 bregenz-hannover, de
                                          date: 17 nov. 10.17
                                 DESTINATION: koblet h, wülfel
                                       velodrome, hannover, de
                                                    Words: 19
                                                      Ös2.28
```

YOU WON – CONGRATS! All arranged. Hotel riva, seestrasse, bregenz. 5*. See you Sunday. Can't wait to see car! W.

22.02.51
Engelhartgasse 6
Hietzing 1130
Vienna
Tel: 2162

Hey!

I am writing to explain what I meant. I understand that your mother wants to meet me, and I guess it's normal. My problem is that, what with our respective careers, we never seem to have any time alone together. I was looking forward to two days without any interference, and I bought the Charlie Parker LP you were telling me about. I was just wanting to "kick back" (as our American friends would say) and that's why I was a bit taken aback when you said you wanted to bring her to Vienna. That's no reflection on your mum. I'm sure she's lovely (she's your mum, after all) but just because our time together is precious.

Anyway I suppose I'm going to have to get used to sharing you, and we'll have a WONDERFUL time anyway. See you next week!

1000 xxx

Dear Hugo

25.06.51

Swiss Cycling
Federation,
Schulstrasse 798,
7555 Brügg

Hugo Koblet
Hildastrasse 3
Zurich

Dear Koblet,

Let me begin with your second place at the Tour de Suisse in general, and the penultimat stage to Davos in particular. I never saw crowwds like it at a Swiss race. Of course that's a testimony to you and Kübler and to the work me and my team have been carrying out. Your attack on the Bernina Pass was inspiring, but please don't forget that the success you and Kübler are enjoying is only possible because of the work we do here. It was good for the Swiss public to see two Swiss grand tour winners on Flüela Pass.

It can't have been easy for you to accept the defeat but it was important that you rode the lap of honopur together because two champions are always better than one. These gestures are important for the federation as we search for the new sponsors to help us maintain a healthy balance sheet.

Regarding the Tour the "situation" is that Kübler won't participate. He is focused on the World Championshipso you will lead the Swiss team in France. You can only have seven domestiques eeven though Bobet and Copppi will each have eleven. It's not ideal but Pélissier will provide everything you will need and if you conduct yourself correctly you have a chance.

Yours in sport
Karol Sennheiser, President.

```
                                    TELEGRAM CERT. 1951 XiiI
                                           POST OFFICE milan
              DESTINATION: CYCLIST KOBLET, tour de france, brive
                                           Sender: Guerra L. 975464
                                                ISSUEr: milan sw1
                                                        WORDS: 23
                                     DATE/TIME: 14 JUly 1951. 16.49
```

Congrats on tt-40.5kmh! Coppi broken - in mourning for serse. Bobet bad legs. Smash them now. Don't wait for Pyrenees. Repeat – don't wait!
learco

```
------------------------------------------------
                ITINERARY AUGUST 1951
------------------------------------------------

                 Post-Tour Criteriums

            Koblet (N.B. maillot jaune obligatory

                FF2000 per race plus primes

                       CASH ONLY


2/8     Aarau
3/8     Cavaillon
4/8     Delgess
5/      Pleurtuit
6/8     Plougonven
7/8     Arras (14.00) Amiens (omnium with Geminiani, Bobet Lazaridès) (18.30)
8/8     Rouen
10/8    Redon
11/8    Angers
12/8    Ussel (13.00) Tulle (18.00)
13/8    Lyon 19.30 (omnium with Coppi and Bobet)
14/8    Ceynon 16.00 (omnium with Bobet, Ockers, Ruiz)
15/8    Troyes
16/8    Tarbes 13.00 (omnium with Coppi and Bobet) Moub
17/8    Carcassone  11.00 Agen 16.00 Marmande 19.3
18/8    Brive 13.00 Aurillac 18.00
20/8    Antwerp (13.30) Ghent (omnium tbc 18.00)
21/8    Lille (possible omnium - tbc) Ypres 18.30
TBC     Issoire, Boussac Ajain + BrusSels

------------------------------------------------
```

10.08.51

SPEERT COMBS
Crafted in Zurich
Since 1778
Lindenstrasse 53,
8008, Zurich. Tel:
53.12.86

Hugo Koblet
Hildastrasse 3
8004
Zurich

Dear Mr Koblet,

I saw the report about the stage to Agen at the Cinema, and like everyone else I read about it in the 'paper. To hold off Magni, Coppi, Bartali and Bobet for 140 kilometres on the flat seemed impossible. To put time into them seemed superhuman, and still more so because it seems they were all contributing.

I was delighted to note that the comb you used at the finish was one of ours. We at Spicher are honoured by that because, like you, we are proud to be of Zurich.

My question, therefore, is whether we might formalize a sponsorship arrangement? We will provide a range of combs and a financial consideration, and all you need do is continue to use them.

If you are amenable to the idea, please let me know at your earliest convenience. I would be delighted to buy you lunch, and to provide a draft proposal.

Yours sincerely,
Fritz Spicher

19.08.51

A MONTADORI
PUBLISHING WEEKLY
Milan

Hugo Koblet
Hildastrasse 3
8004
Zurich
Switzerland

Dearest Hugo,

I hope this finds you well. As promised a copy of the magazine, hoping that it pleases you.

As a "serious" current affairs publication we'd never featured any sportsmen on the cover before. I don't deny that there was some consternation when I announced what we were doing, but sport is important and ultimately a Tour de France-winning "Pédaleur de Charme" was irresistible. Besides there's a first time for everything, and it seems to have been wildly successful. Sales have been outstanding, and I'm hearing that it's been successful with the female audience. We've had an upsurge in subscriptions, so... thanks!

Finally, best of luck at the World Championships.

Your sincerely,
Alberto Montadori

Dear Hugo

07.10.51

South Bend, Indiana
USA

Hugo Koblet
Hildastrasse 3
Zurich
Switzerland

Dear Mr Koblet,

We recently had word from our European distributor that you purchased one of our vehicles. I've heard all about your victory at the "Tour du Francaise" and it seems like you guys have a whole lot of fun.

We in South Bend are honoured that one of the world's top cyclers has chosen a Studebaker, and extend an open invitation to visit us whenever you please.

I assume all that pedalling is thirsty work so I enclose a small token of our appreciation.

Yours faithfully,
Harold Vanse (President)

17th June 2021

I'd been obsessed by cycling since the afternoon id'd "met" Hugo, But now everyone else seemed obsessed too. I think it was because we Swiss had never had anything like that before. We weren't used to famous sportspeople (because in cycling it had always been the French, the Belgians and the ITALlians.Now suddenly we had two Tour de France winners!

Everyone was talking about them because when there was a big race one of them always seemed to win..Ferdi won the Fleche Wallonne and Liege-Bastogne-Liége in the same weekend. He was the best in the world at the single day races but Hugo went and beat him at the GP Zurich.

I hardly sleaped at all during the 1951 Tour because there was so much going on and I found it all abit ovwerwhelming. I had my birthday in the middle of it, on 15 July! In the morning we went to Amberg's shop and I got a real racing bike of my own. I'd been saving for the deposit and he said I could pay a bit each week just so long as I paid on time and didn't try any funny business. I told him I a Learco Guerra bike like the Giro one, or a LA PErle like the one Koblet was riding at the Tour. Leo said he didn't have them and Swiss bikes were the best anyway. He was a champion cyclist and a friend of my dad, so of course i believed him. He showed me a used CILO the same colours as Koblet's. It was beautiful and dad said he'd help me to pay for it if I was serious and took vcare of it. I told Leo I'd already applied for my racing license because I'd been waiting 4 years! Co

19th June 2021

The birthday stage was Brive to Agen and it's very important if you want to know what I think. Sugar Ray Robinson was there meeting the riders.. He was a famous boxer, and of course my dad knew all about him. There was a big photo of him in the news-papaer meeting Koblet and Schär, and that was quite funny because Schär was a tiny guy who could shoot up mountains fatsrer than Robic.
I spent the afternoon listening to the radio and when Hugo attacked they said they didn't understand him. They said he was crazy to do that with 135 kilo-metres still to race on a flat stage. Theyk kept saying he was too impulsive and it was a waste of energy but it turned out they were wrong and he wasn't crazy at all. The commentator was crazy and the Italians and FREnch went crazy, because they couldn't

Dear Hugo

catch him and they never saw him again. There were 100 of them and 1 of him, and he still put 3 minutes into them! The Weilenmann brothers were in the group which trying to catch him (they didn't contribute obviously because they were his friends and Swiss and they knew that the better he did the more they would earn - that was how it worked), Anyway Leo Weilenmann said the last 40 kilometres was furyous. They said Coppi, Lazarides, Magni, Ockers and Gemigniani were doing big turns and still they couldn't bring him back.. They said it should have been impossible to stay away with the Italians and the French pulling like that but somehow he did it. They said it was the greatest thing they ever witnessed in a bike race and think that's why its become so famous.it was as if Hugo was cycling in a different dimension or something. I'd say it was as if he was a prince and the rest were paupers, or as if he was floating and they were plodding along because they were just normal human beings and he was a God.

    When dad got home we a party. Mum had made a special birthday cake with a marzipan yellow jersey on it.Aftwerwards in my room I tried to work out all the calculations and permutashions. Hugo had 3 minutes on Gemigniani, 6 on Bobet and 7 on Coppi. I was worried about Coppi, but not about the others because I knew tjhey'd all lose at least 5 minutes in the time trial. In the end it didn't matter theough because it was already over by the time trial. Coppi had his defaillance on the stage to Montpellier and lost 30 minutes. I suppose I was happy about that even though I liked Coppi because it meant that Hugo only had to not crash or have a terrible day and he would win the Tour de France. The thing I remember about that was that Hugo wasn't really happy at all. Coppi had always been his idol a and now he'd become his friend you see?. He was having a very bad time because his brother (he was called Serse and he wasa domestqie) had died and Hugo was more concerened about that than the yellow jersey. That's what he was like. He was a true sportsman.

    Afterwards I explained to my dad why I was of the opinion that he was better than Coppi. I showed gim a table I'd made which proved that Koblet was better at sprinting and time trialing and much better at descending. My dad said Hugo had only won two of the seven sisters (they were the big races) and it it was difficult to be sure with this

Tour because of the situation with Serse. We agreed that they were much better than the others and we'd see who was the best time trialist at Lugano and Grand Prix des Nations. For the Giro and the Tour we'dd just have to wait until the following year.

~~21th June 2021~~   M̶y̶

21st June 2021

After the Tour de France my dad and I went to the San Bernadino stage of the Tour de Suisse. They say ity was the best Tour de Suisse ever and it was surely one of the best days we had together at the cycling. Hugo won the stage and Ferdi the overall. Then later Ferdi went an won the world championship in Varese and I remember because me and my dad looked at one another in our cycling code. We both knew we'd made a mistake by not going, you see, because it would have been quite easy to get the train to Chiasso and then on to Varese. ANYway there was a big parade when the Swiss team came home and Kobletand Kübler embraced one another.

    Then we went to the meeting at the Oerlikon with Hugo in the yellow jerssey and Ferdi in the rainbow. You couldn't move in there that day because it was packed and they say 20,000 people were locked outside.

    I want to explain something about Ferdi and Hugo because people who weren't there don't always understand it. It's true that they were diffferent characters and they had different supporters. k0blet fans like me tended to be younger and a bit more modern. We tried to be "cool" and to dress like Hugo. I even bought some jazz records from Müller's down town, and I pretended I liked them even though most of them sounded terrible to me. my mum couldn't understand it at all but later, before she died, she told me she'd known all along I was just trying to fit in. I told everyone I was a fan of Charlie Parker. I never actually played his record because I didn0t like it. It was an alto saxophone you see and it sounded like a cat squealing to me.. I made sure I knew the names of all the songs though because I thought if I acted sofisticcated I would have had something in common with Hugo. It was silly of course but I was young and I was searching for an identity of my own.

Dear Hugo

The serious bike riders and fashioners went to Hans Martin's cafe on Schützen-Gasse which was just in front of the station. It was sort of a Koblet fan club because he used to go there to play Jass and Martin was his friend. People went there because they wanted to meet him and I wanted to as well. The problem with that was there was alcohol and I wasn't old enough so I couldn't go in. From time to time I'd stand on the corner and watch in secret. I tried to pretend I wasn't there but I neededd to see what they wore, how they moved and the way they smoked their cigarettes.

I rememeber this one guy who looked a lot like Hugo. He was tall and blonde, and he would always pull out his comb when a beautiful girl came by, like Hugo did after the races. I was a bit jealous of him so I bought a comb and tried to organize my hair like he did. I remember I even got some "hair tonic". I had no idea what it was for, but it was made by Cheseline and they sponsored Hugo. I put it on my hair one evening but then my dad came in the room and saw me. He told my mum about it and she told me I wasn't allowed to use it at school. With the cigarettes I didn't know what to do so I thought of burying them somewhere becau- se you see I wasn't supposed to have tjhem?. In the end I hid them in a shoe-box I had under the bed. It was full of old toys and nobody looked in it. Then I went on the bus to the industrial estate one saturday afternoon when nobody was there. I wanted to learn to smoke and I knew nobody would see me there. I thought I dideverything right but I hated it and anyway it didn't work because it made my head spin. I gave up and decided smoking was not for me. Anyway Hugo Koblet didn't smoke so why should I?

....

25th June 2021

I had to take a few days off the writing becauuse have it's tiring and sometimes I get upset going over things. I have to try to remember things as they were so it's better if I don't just rush ahead. Anyway the Küblians would met in a bar right across the street from the Kobletists, and they were a different crowd. Don't get me wrong because I liked Kübler. I liked all the swiss rider s but Ferdis supporters tended to be a bit older and more traditional. They were people like my dad and my uncle. I think they liked him in the countryside and the rural cantons because he was old-fashioned and so were they. They tendedto have to have bourgeois ideas but it was all fine and I tried to get along with everyone.

I should mention that the K&K sponsors were rivals as well. Ferdi rode for Tebag and they made their bikes here in Zurich. Hugo rode a Cilo bike and they made them down in Lausanne and the thing is they speak French down there. I told my dad that was fine because Hugo and Ferdi had each won the Tour de France after all! They had their own groups but as far as I could tell they were always correct. That was important for we Swiss and it's one of ther things they still talk aobout today. It's no use pretending that Ferdi and Hugo were natural friends because they weren't.

I joined the cycling club and sent applicatins to as many races as I could. It wasn't easy because cycling was really popular. I remember getting on a train to Basel with my bike one Sunday, because the races near us were all ffull. I rem-ember because I was number 249 and there were 250 starters.I loved the racing, and I suppose started to get pretty good at it.

....

26th June 2021

A neighbour of ours, mr K , had a haulage business and my dad told me to go and see him. I went round there and he told me he needed someonbe young and strong to help with the loading. I started work for him at 7.15 on 17 September 1951. I suppose you could say that was the end of my childhood.

Dear Hugo

20.09.51

The Mexican
ambassador of The
Swiss Confederation
Calle Sierra Nevada
333, Lomas de
Chapultepec, 11550,
Mexico

Hugo Koblet
Hildastrasse 3
8004
Zurich

Dear Hugo,

I trust you are well as you approach at the conclusion of this long and extremely successful season. I was heartily pleased to read about Kübler's rainbow jersey, but also your victory at the Gran Prix des Nations. I was in conversation with my Italian counterpart, Ambassador Petrucci. He is a sports fan, and he concurred that your beating Coppi in a 140km time trial is perhaps the greatest of all your achievements.

    Regarding your proposed visit, I have the details from Esto, the newspaper which organizes the Tour of Mexico. The race begins on 24 November, and there will be 13 or 14 stages. In short the race organizer, Valseca, wishes to extend a formal invitation for the duration of the race. As guest of honour you will be expected to attend diplomatic events, and inevitably the host cities will organize a flurry of social gatherings. You will provide analysis of the route and riders, and to be on hand for the ceremonies. The Mexicans are keen to develop as a cycling nation, and to liaise regarding new velodromes, races and suchlike. It's also possible they may prevail upon you for a "demonstration ride", though I've stressed that you will be recuperating. For their part, they will make available a villa, a Cadillac (with chauffer) and a personal bodyguard for the duration of your stay.

    In addition, Teddy "The Swing King" Stauffer is proposing an all-inclusive break at his deluxe resort in Acapulco after the race. As you probably know, Teddy recently married Hedy Lamarr, the so-called "World's most beautiful woman". She's extremely popular here, and I'm told "Samson and Delilah" has broken box-office records in Mexico as well as America. It seems they want to introduce you to Cecil B. Demille, and other cinematic luminaries. If you choose to accept it could be a good opportunity, and I'm sure you'll have a wonderful time down there.

    Please confirm by return. If you are in agreement I will expedite the visa application, and have them formalize your travel arrangements.

Yours sincerely,

Amb. Edoaurd de Bouvoir

24.09.51
LA SENTINELLE
Les Nouvelles
de Demain,
Aujourd'hui!

Rue de Commerce 11,
2000, Neuchâtel.
Tel: 32 701 9906

Hugo Koblet
Hildastrasse 3
8004
Zurich

Dear Koblet,

Forgive my having written unsolicited, but I heard your interview on SRF, and I wanted to clarify a couple of issues. You stated that our headline and coverage for Kübler's having won the Tour was much bigger than for your victory. I have thoroughly checked the respective editions of the 'paper, and I wanted to share my findings.

It's true that there's slightly more coverage for Ferdi's Tour, but there are circumstantial reasons. There were important athletics events taking place the day you won, and we had a duty to report them. That doesn't diminish what you accom-plished, but it remains a matter of fact. There were no other significant sporting events the day Kübler won the Tour, and so we cut our editorial cloth accordingly.

You made mention of the higher quality riders you had to overcome, and that the defection of the Italians facilitated Ferdi's win. This is correct, but some would point to Coppi's situation and suggest that he wasn't perhaps at his best this year. None of this diminishes what you accomplished, but nor should we underestimate Ferdi's achievements. He had to overcome Ockers, Bobet and Geminianì, and they're very good riders. Besides, that's the nature of sport, and it's the reason we love it.

In closing, I want to assure you that our 'paper will continue to report cycling objectively and fairly. We understand that you and Kübler are totally different both as riders and as people. You are, as the Italians say, "the sun and the moon", but you are both Swiss and you may be assured that we at La Sentinelle will report your careers even-handedly.

I sincerely hope this helps to set your mind at rest.

Walter Bickel
Editor-in-chief, sports.

Dear Hugo

> Hugo, BY HAND
>
> I know you think I'm a pain but I'm your friend as well as your racing partner. If I can't tell you what I think then nobody will.
>
> When I heard that Hans had hired a Fairchild to fly you around the post-Tour criteriums, I kept my mouth shut. I thought it was CRAZY to spend all that money, but I supposed it was easier than driving yourself. You say "You only live once " and I know you have trouble saying "no" to people. That's as maybe, but you should listen sometimes! You should have rested before the Worlds. Bevilacqua is decent but he's not in your class if you train propperly. You don't like it but Ferdi won the RAINBOW JERSEY on the road because he was SERIOUS. You threw yours away for the sake of a few lousy criteriums, and I'll never understand that. You fly to Morocco and Algeria to do crazy stuff, but he's here training propperly and resting. I can see it upsets you that Ferdi is more popular but it's not hard to understand. You've ridden 150 days this year, and now you say you're away off to MEXICO to meet people from Hollywood! Swiss people aren't used to that sort of thing. They don't understand it. See you when you get back,
>
> Armin.

08.11.51

Headquarters: 515 E24th Street, Hope, Kansas

Hugo Koblet
Hildastrasse 3
8004
Zurich
Switzerland

Dear Mr. Koblet,
We enclose your first-class tickets to Mexico City, with stopover at New York.

Your itinerary:

19 Nov:	Dep: Kloten Zurich	09.40 GMT+1
	Arr: LaGuardia New York	19.40 EDT
	Dep: LaGuardia New York	22.30 EDT
	Arr: Mexico City Int	07.40 CDT

A driver will collect you from your home at 07.00 on 19 November. Ambassador de Bouvoir's driver will make himself known to you when you land in Mexico City.

MEET THE TOUR DE FRANCE WINNER

HUGO KOBLET,
PEDALLER OF CHARM!

CHAMPAGNE RECEPTION,
HYATT REGENCY, ACAPULCO

RSVP to:
MGM-PARAMOUNT, tel: 55.976
teddy & hedy, tel: 55.451

DRESS CODE
STRICTLY COCKTAIL, STRICTLY
LUSCIOUS...

Hotel Isabel

AN IDEAL PLACE FOR TOURISTS

ISABEL LA CATOLICA 63 APARTADO 7249
CABLE: ISABELOTEL: MEXICO, D.F.

MEXICO, D.F.

*You looked so beautiful sleeping.
I didn't want to wake you...*

Ciaoooooo!

> Howdy Hugo, BY HAND
>
> He had a wonderful day with you. He keeps on asking when you will come back! Thanks for the gifts you brought him from "Mexco". I will make sure he's a good "Ombre" in his hat! He wears it every day to practice his shooting. He says he wants to come over to see his "Partner" uncle Gütti! He keeps asking when he will have a cousin so they can play together and live in "Merika" like real cowboys! He says he loves you very much!
>
> dolf

29.12.51
Zurich Private
Clinic, Dr. Marius
Favre, Senior
Urologist
Sustenstrasse 129,
8048 Zurich

Patient: Koblet H, Hildastrasse 3
Syphillis infection – Total rest
500mg penicillin x4 daily, 7 days.
Appt. 05-01-52, 11 o'clock
M. Favre

26.02.52

Obergass 3,
Eglisau. Tel: 841

Hugo Koblet
Hildastrasse 3
8004
Zurich

Dear Hugo,

I do hope you're well, and recovering from Wednesday's thrilling omnium. Erika informs me that you haven't banked the last two cheques we sent. I sincerely hope they reached you, and that it's an oversight on your part. Do let me know if you didn't get them?
Best regards,
Emile.

10.06.52
Cicli Guerra
Via Giulio Ferreri
20153
Milano
Tel: 3929

Dear Hugo,

Here is the shoes you left behind at the Giro. I think we can agree that it wasn'yt a success. Without preparataion it's not possible at this level for three weks. It was importnt to arrive in top condition we saw this.
It's normal that Coppi won but not normal to lose 3 minutes in a 35km crono. I believe 8 position isn't correct for a rider like you. You would need to think about how you want

Dear Hugo

for your career to go. If you don't ride on the rest day you will pay. If you eat ice cream you will pay. If you don't do cycling seriously you will pay. You know all these things. It's for you to decide.

I'm coming to the TdS so I'll see you at the start in Zurich.

Best,
Learco

17.06.52

Swiss Cycling Federation,
Schulstrasse 798,
7555 Brügg

Hugo Koblet
Hildastrasse 3
Zurich

Dear Koblet,

I received a letter from your doctor Ruft, and was somewhat aggrieved by the tone. whilst I'm sure he has your best int-erst at heart, the language is accusatory and that will not stand.

There's no value in raking over it all, but I remind you that You'd been riding well in the preceding stages. It seemed normal and I mmaintain that what happened in that room was done in the best interests of our cycling movement. We all rely on sponsors, and we all know how important the TdS is. The public wants to see you and Kübler most of all. It was right that you went on.

Ruft suggested that you were "sabotaged" and "doped", but he needs to think carefully about the language he adopts. Doctor Grüss is a good man, and we were all in agreement – yourself included – that the injection was worth a try. Maybe it doidn't have the desired effect, but we couldn't have known that and at least it got you to the start line for th time trial. It's easy Ruft to make wild accusations, but Ruft CLEARly doesn't understand cycling and he doesn't have an entire movement on his shouldders.

I wish you a speedy recovery, and trust that this is an end to the matter. Nobody will benefit from it becoming public, and I repeat that you consented to the treatment. In order to avoid a damaging escalation, please keep your counsel and invite Doctor Ruft to do likewise.

Sincerely,
Sennheiser.

```
                                      MODULE 6/13445 1952 VI
                                             TELEGRAM OFFICE
                DESTINATION: KOBLET, HILDASTRASSE 3 dist. 4
                                     ISSUED BY: Zurich dist.9
                                                977 ZURICH-ZURICH
                                                         19.06.52
                                                         SD90832.
                                                            11.11
```

SPOKE WITH PROF. LöFFLER – ALSO EXTREMELY CONCERNED ABOUT AORTIC VALVE. URGENT – WILL PICK YOU UP AT 4.

```
23.06.52
L'EQUIPE
THE SPORT DAILY

Hugo Koblet
Hildastrassse 3
Zurich
Switzerland
```

Dear Koblet,

How terribly sad! The Tour is "televised" for the first time, and our "Pedaller of Charm" won't be present for this new dawn. All the world was so looking forward to a great coming together between yourself and Coppi.

Alas, alas…

We'll reconvene next year – be well!

Gaudet.

To KOBLET!!
Raced suter and and perriere i did look it up !!
 second at birsfalden i was everyone remembers that day,, why i supporting ferdinand Kübler!? more to life than fornickating !!! you a fancy zuricher drinking shandy cock-tales off talking funny foreigner languages and jazzy music swiss wireless not good enough for you KOBLET!! movie actress from Austria mr shandy-pants KOBLET? swiss wenches not better!!!! KOBKLET! hate us enyhow them there. Just after money all the same! makes my piss boil think on young KOBLET!!!

From CHOPARD .

Dear Hugo

H,   BY HAND

About last week in Dortmund. It was good but for every 10 marks we earned, you spent 11. You spent half your money on ONE RAINCOAT even though you admitted you already have a dozen raincoats. You insisted that we eat at the Brauhaus. She told you she had a boyfriend and wasn't interested and still you kept on giving her too large tips! Every time you said "keep the change" and "it's only a few pfennigs" But it adds up. For the petrol station guy 18 marks - he only asked for an autograph! god only knows how much to those velodrome kids - 5 for you, 3 for him, 4 for the other one and his friend. Here there and everywhere - Hugo's money for everyone! They aren't your FRIENDS Hugo and you DON'T need to give them money! You say you're only going to do another couple of years on the road, and you want to take a wife, have kids and "travel the world". Well YOU will need MONEY for that!
think about what I said? You still don'thave a bank account! It's not normal to go around with a trunk full of money and sooner or later someone will steal it - of course they will. What harm can it do to open an account like normal people? All you have to do is walk in and ask them. It takes 10 minutes.

Armin

Dr. Ernst Platter
Consultant Pathologist
Sumatrasrasse 16, 8006 Zurich. Tel: 778.128

Hugo Koblet
Hildastrassse 3
8004
Zurich
Switzerland

22 August 1952

Dear Mr Koblet,

I've spoken with Dr. Ruft. If, as he is suggesting, you are experiencing abdominal pains, you should desist from all physical activity forthwith. It goes without saying that compromised red blood cell production isn't consistent with athletic performance, so we need to analyze and address the issue poste-haste.

Please present yourself here at the clinic on Monday morning at 9AM. Once we have the test results back from the laboratory, we will establish the right course of action.

Yours sincerely,

Platter

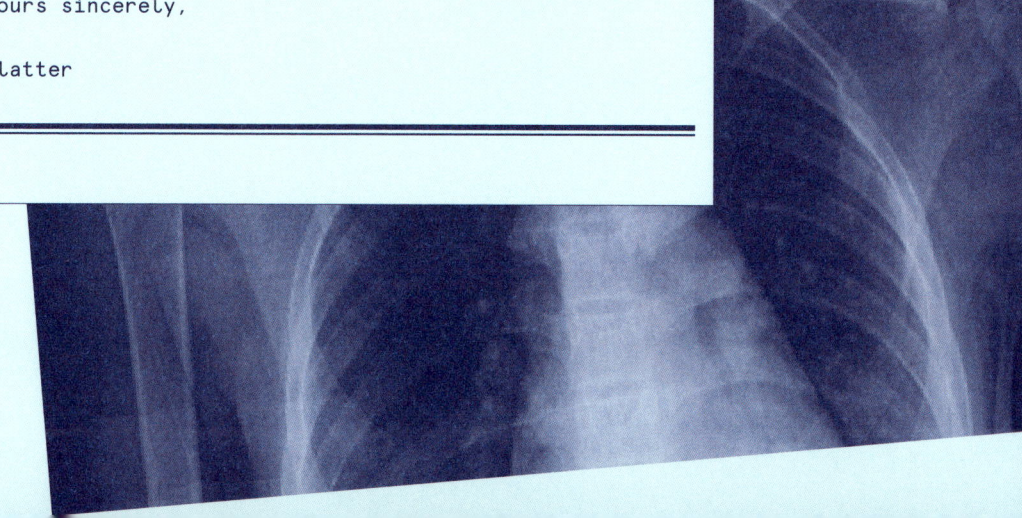

ZURICH POLICE PRECINCT SIX
CRIME REPORT

Case No: 156874　　　　　　　　Date: 11 May 1953, 2.37 pm
Officer: Kramer　　　　　　　　Prepared By: Kramer

Incident:
The victim's house at 3 Hildastrasses was the subject of a break-in between the hours 00 and 09.00, resulting in the theft of the following items:
  1x Solid silver Tour de France trophy
  1x Giro d'Italia trophy with shield and goblets
  1x gold Tour de Suisse trophy
  Several other trophies, medals, plaques and suchlike related to cycling. About 10 "special" cycling jerseys from the Tour de France, Giro d'Italia, Tour de Suisse, Tour of Romadie etc.
  Ten wrist watches
  Various other jewellry and other valuables belonging to the victim's mother, including earrings, a gold necklace and an emerald ring.
  About 50,000 Swiss francs in cash, as well as "very large" cash sums of German Deutschmarks, French francs and Italian lire. The victims estimates their Swiss franc eqivalent at 75,000

Detail of Event:
The victim was at a prize-giving event for the Tour of Romandie bicycle race, which he won. He arrived home shortly after 9 o'clock this morning and discovvered that somebody had forced the lock. The house had been "turned upside down" and everything of value had been taken. Items removed from the property included all his cups and medals, and a considerable cash sum. (The victim states that most of his earning are retained as cash).

H,

good to see my old classmates again after all these years.

Thanks for lending me the cash - you're a life saver.

You know I'll pay you back as soon I get things sorted, hopefully next month.

Still don't have the new address, but I'll send when I have it.

```
15.06.53
Cicli Guerra
Via Giulio Ferreri
20153, Milano
Tel: 3929

Hugo Koblet
Hildastrassse 3
Zurich
Switzerland
```

Dear Hugo,

I had to keep a bit more because there is new taxes. Please don't say you won't ride Giro again. Italians can be arseholes its true bu think seriously because it's possible to arrange everything better. It not important what Fausto did —he has had 60 gregari at this Giro and they must all look at themselves in the mirror. Bianchi can afford them and I can't – that's everytthing. They are wankers and in the end I told them to fuck off because you did a great Giro and I told Fausto what he did was not acceptable. I feel bad that you were always on your own but I can't spend money I haven't got. Ask Clerici to take swizss nationality. He's a good boy and they treated him terrible at this Giro. you can't expel a guy out of the Giro just because he helps a friend – it's normal!!. Clerici is more swiss than Italian anyway because he's of Zurich like you. Try to talk with him and tell him if he becomes Swiss he can come with us next year. We will treat him good.

Anyway you can win the Tour again. there's not a problem if you stay healthy and don't do stupidity. be careful dexscending and don't exaggerate. I'm certain of it.

Sorry again.

```
26.06.53
Fausto Coppi
Novi Ligure
```

Dear Hugo,

I'm writing about the Giro, because you refusef d to ride with me or speak to me at the Vigorelli. You think I tricked you so I want to try to explain myself. When we made our pact for me to win the stages in BBormio and Bolzano, it was partly because of my "situation". It's been hard since Serse died and life at home has been unbeearable. I want to be happy like everyone else with this one I finally feel like I can have some fun. I 'm not interested in spending my life with her but she's a different to Bruna and she's very good at certain "things. I knew she was coming to Bormio and I'd been rooming with Milano for three weeks! I thought if I won the stage and gave her the dflowers she might… show her aoo ppreciation.

If I'm honest I didn't think I could drop you on the Stelvio anyway so it seemed like the correct thing – for

Dear Hugo

you the Giro and for me the two stages. I want you to know
that I meant what I said, at least when I said it. You were
stronger than me at this Giro, and you rode it more or less
on your own.

You deserved to win but my problem is all the people
I have depending on me. The gregari, Bianchi, Tragella,
Campagnolo, The Gazzetta, sponsors... Sometimes I wish
they'd all just leave me alone but II had to be seen to at least
try to drop you. I honestly thhought you'd catch me on the
descent anyway and you seemed to be riding very smoothly.
I should have waited and I would have waited if I'd known
you were struggling. I thought I only had about a minute (I
didn't know you'd punctured) and I was horrified when you
didn't come and they told me I was maglia rosa beccause it
really wasn't my intention. When you refused to ride the
madison with me on nMonday it made me reflect. I did a
bad thing, so all I can do is beg your forgiveness and hope
we can be friends again. Do respond if you are able.

Fausto.

P.S. Congrar t ulations on the Tour de Suisse – Defilippis
told me what you did was incredible! I'm not coming to
the Tour. I don't have the frame of mind, so I'm going to
stay here and prepare for the Worlds instead. If you ride
within yourself and don't take any risks, you will win it
by half an hour.

12.07.53
Engelhartgasse 6
Hietzing 1130
Vienna
Tel: 2162

Hugo Koblet
Hildastrasse 3
8004
Zurich
Switzerland

Dearest Hugo,

I'm sorry about the Tour, and still more so that you pushed
me away like that. I would have liked to talk things
through, but I think we both know that things aren't
working. Our careers are important, and I'm not prepared
to give mine up at the moment. Besides, you've been pretty
detached lately, as if you're trying to tell me something
without saying it?

Time to move on with our lives.
It's been nice but... so long, cowboy.

W

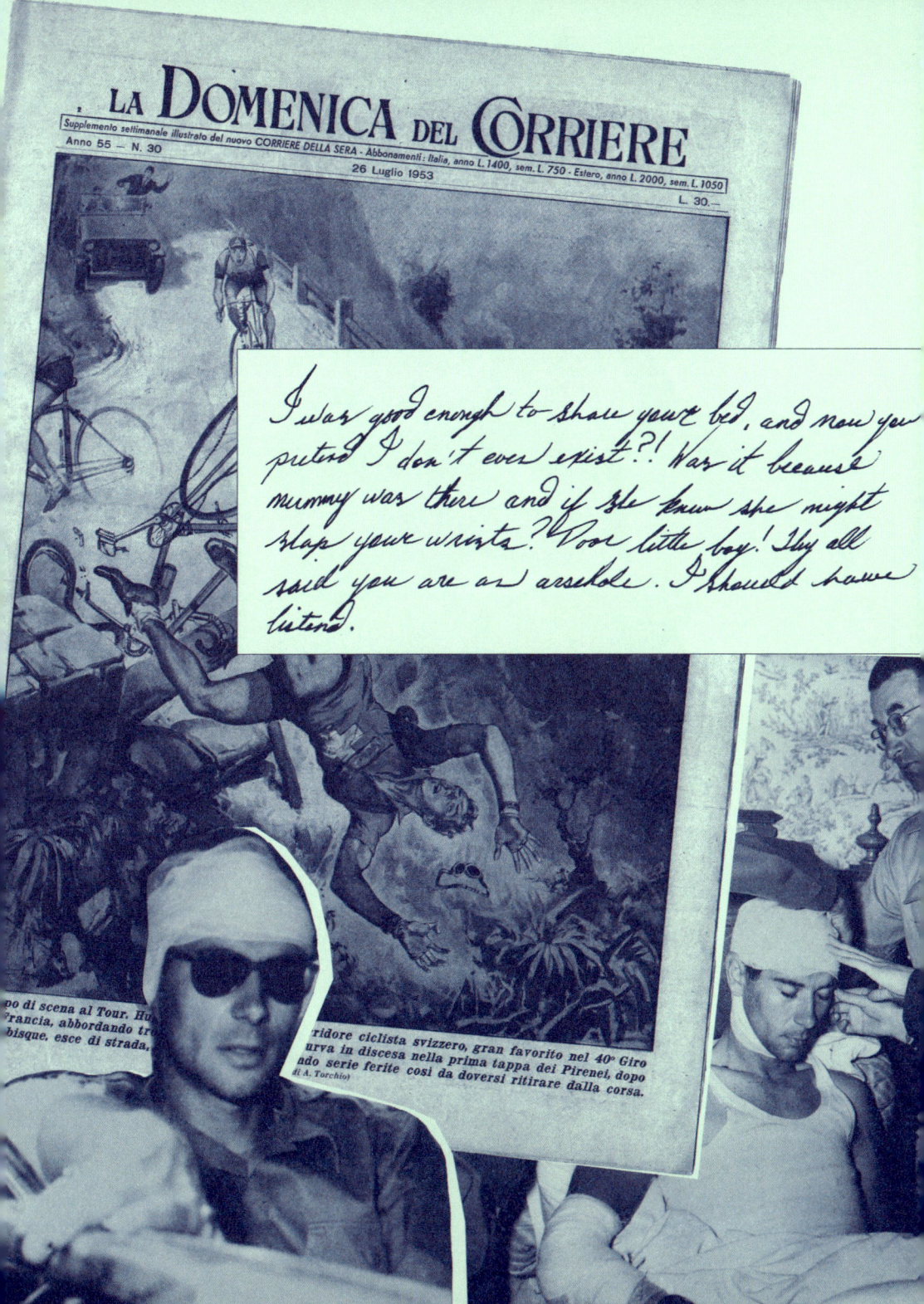

```
                                           MODULE 6/13445 1953 VI
                                                  TELEGRAM OFFICE
                               DESTINATION: KOBLET, HILDASTRASSE 3
                                      ISSUED BY: RUFT/Zurich dist.9
                        977 ZURICH-ZURICH SD96776. 17 JULy  1953. 18.42
                                                         WORDS: 18
```

IT SEEMS THE THE THIGH NEEDS AN OP' HUGO – I AM SORRY. hirslanden clinic TOMORROW AT 10. GENi

```
02.02.54
Hallenstadion
Velodrome
Wallisellenstrasse
45, 8050, Zurich

Hugo Koblet
Hildastrasse 3
8004
Zurich
```

Dear Hugo,

I write to confirm that, following a meeting with the organizing committee, we shall be proceeding with the inaugural Six Days of Zurich here at the Hallenstadion beginning 23 March. I have spoken with Van Büren with respect to your appearance fees, and agreement has been reached.

As of today we have pledges totalling in excess of 25,000 francs in prize money, and Emil Frey has agreed to donate a car as a special sprint prize on the Friday evening. We expect healthy attendances and bar sales, not least because you and Van Büren will be present and we anticipate thrilling racing. Both Schulte-Peters and Bucher-Roth will appear, but you will be assigned jersey number 1 as befits your local status and international Reputation.

The consensus of the committee was that the Zurich public has no wish to see "fake" racing, and that the stimulants which have become all too commonplace on the Six-Day circuit have no place here. With this in mind – and with the interests of the riders' well-being foremost - we have decided to dispense with the traditional format. Whilst the riders may not leave the velodrome for the duration, there will be no racing between 0500 and 1300 hours. We recognise that this is a radical departure, but ours is a new Six-Day and we feel there is nothing to be gained by simultan-eously depriving you of sleep and neutralizing the racing, and we feel sure that the event will be more dynamic as a consequence.

I will furnish more details as I have them.
Emil Keller

Dear Hugo

15.02.54
Cicli Guerra
Via Giulio Ferreri
20153
Milano
Tel: 3929

Hugo Koblet
Hilda strassse
number 3
Zurich
Switzerland

Dear Hugo,

Tell Clerici to take swizss nationality. He's a good boy and they treated him terrible last year at Giro. You can't expel a guy out of the Giro just because he helps a friend of his – it's normal!!. Clerici is more swizss than Italian anyhow he's of Zurich. You his friend and he cares a lot. Try to talk with him and tell him to become swizss because like that he can come with us. we will treat him good and he will be a very good gregario. Learco

---

09.03.54   BY HAND
Walter Bilk
Magazingasse 14,
Liestal

Hugo Koblett
Hildastrasse Bakers shop
Zurich

Dear Mr Hugo Koblett,

   I am Walter Bilk. I'm 12 and from Liestal and I also plan to be a champion cyclist when I get everything sorted out. I got a bike because they were saying I was chubby and whatnot so uncle told me it was a good way to slim down and what have you. I alreaddy started and my best result was 43rd which is fine and I'm only just starting my career.still still a touch on the heavy side of things if you see what I mean.. My dad told me you won your first road race since the Tour when you fell off. I know that's 9 months ago (counted them). So anyway I thought id write you a letter which is what I'm doing now. I was wondering if maybe you could write back signed by you with some tips about trying to improve and whatnot. that would be best and I bet if I went to school with a letter from Hugo Koblett they'd stop teasing me just because I'm a little on the heavy side. I already eat less cakes and I have tickets for the six day because I want to meet the real you not just a →

→ photo in a magazine and whatnot. The stamp is already on the envelope so when you finish writing the letter just pop it in and go to the postbox and don't worry because it won't take long. The reason is because my uncle says you're proberbly busy cycling and what have you. By the way you can do a postcard to him with your autograf on it if you like. You can write to my good friend Hans Bilk from Hugo Koblett or something like that. thanks Mr Koblett and by the way best wishes for Paris-Roobeys and what have you. Yours sincerely and faithfully from the cyclist Walter Bilk of Liestal.

07.04.54
Cicli Guerra
Via Giulio Ferreri
20153
Milano
Tel: 3929

Dearest Uhgo,

Everything is in place with the federatioon. SORry the money a bit less this time but in italy they all want scooters nowI asked Ursus for more but he says it's on its arse and he doesn't have. However you will be amuch better and you will be strong like Bianchi . There are more intermediate sprints sowe can invent something. The situation of Fausto and that woman is very delicate now. I think he's not serene and we can profit. Clerici = OK. xx See you all in Palermo 19 May. Hotel Garibaldi in Via Settimo. Learco

---

to KOBLET Zurich

Cycling before you was born me!!the brother rode the tour with lapize and faber stage was 424km caen it was! Not for the riting left school when was 8 poor we was there was the animals needed tending!! you from Zurich probbly never killed a pig long days KOBLET!! WORK

    Mathilde done this on the riting masceene like it or lump it KOBLET!... yyou got some big americkan car driving round zurich they say what for is what i say?? why you even need car you have a bike i say ?mtypical zuricher full of fancy ways always the same!.,. brother had trouble with his other leg you can ask anyone gout it was if he wasn't dead hed say you a idiot uncle gustaaf 54 he was typhus think on young KOBLET!!.
Chopard e.!

Dear Hugo

14.11.54
HEINZE, ROTH &
THALMANN
LAND AGENTS
ALTE LANDSTRASSE 4,
KÜSNACHT 8700.

Hugo Koblet
Hildastrasse 3
8004
Zurich

Re: Offer and acceptance: Wassbergstrasse 206, Forch.

Dear Mr. Koblet,
We are delighted to confirm that the vendor has accepted your offer for the property. I enclose the instruction form and a stamped, addressed envelope. Please complete the form and return it to me along with a deposit of 5000 francs in the form of a cashier's cheque. Alternatively you may make a bank transfer as follows:
Farmer's Bank of Lausanne
Acct: CH3357 0001128 0007657 9897423
Beneficiary: Heinze, Roth and Thalmann
Immediately I am in receipt I shall inform the vendor and instruct the notary.
Yours sincerely,
Konrad Roth

19.11.54
HEINZE, ROTH &
THALMANN
LAND AGENTS
ALTE LANDSTRASSE 4,
8700, KÜSNACHT.

Hugo Koblet
Hildastrasse 3
8004
Zurich

Re: Offer and acceptance: Wassbergstrasse 206, Forch.

Dear Mr. Koblet,
I confirm that a cash payment will be acceptable in this instance. I look forward to meeting you on Tuesday morning.
Yours sincerely,
Konrad Roth

22.11.54
Greisz Bros.
The department
store for the
discerning

Mr H. Koblet and
Miss S. Bühl
Hildastrasse 3
8004
Zurich

Dear Mr Koblet and Miss Bühl,
Further to our telephone conversation, it's my pleasure to confirm a private store opening on evening of Monday 30 November. I will meet you at the store entrance at 19.30, and will remain entirely at your disposal for the duration of your visit. Mr Friess will be on hand to assist us during our time in the home furnishings department, Miss Brahms in kitchenware.
 If you have no objection, I should like to promote your visit with instore notices beforehand. That will ensure a healthy audience as you make your entrance on the red carpet, and a photographer will be present to capture the moment. I look forward to welcoming you both next Monday.
Yours sincerely,
Bruno Greisz

HUGO KOBLET

Unser Sieg im Giro

Fr. 1.80

Giro d'Italia 1954

sport illustrato
SETTIMANALE SPORTIVO A COLORI DIRETTO DA EMILIO DE MARTINO

NINO ASSIRELLI
PICCOLO ASSO DI ROMAGNA
HA DIFESO LA BANDIERA ITALIANA

IL BACIO DEL

H,   BY HAND

Hope you had a good time in Madrid pal! Not had much chance to catch up since the wedding mate so I thought I'd write! It was a fantastic day and we're all really pleased you've decided to settle down. We agreed that if there's one cyclist who could marry a catwalk model from a bourgeoise Schaffhausen fsamily, it's you!!

  It was a shame the car broke down but it wasn't your brother's fault and he shouldn't blame himself. Dölf is just one of those unlucky guys, that's all! Anyway you chose well old mate because what I mean is Sonja is a beautiful lady and very classy. Don't tell the wife I said that because you know what she's like! Sonja will have to get used to your working-class ways but she will learn I'm sure of it and anyway you're not exactly rough yourself are you pal?. I imagine you will be ships in the night with her travelling to fashion things and you racing about everywhere! Then again you lost the criteriums when you crashed at the Tour and the money has to come from somewhere! You're always having to help Dölf out and with the bakery closing you'll have your mum to support as well. Looks like you're going to have your hands full but you like being on the move eh pal? I don't mean anything by that by the way.

  I know you prefer riding the track to training on the road and good for you mate is what I say because each to his own and you've done alright for youself . I understand you get money that way as well but long rides help keep the weight down remember!. Even you can't climb the Izoard with Coppi and Bobet if you're too heavy mate – not a chance!. You're always off to Davos or St. Moritz and everyone knows you like the weisswurst too much for your own good!!

  Ferdi admitted it was one of best weddings he's been too even posher than his! Mum's the word but I told him you get what you pay for pal, if you know what I mean ? He showed me his training diary and I don't want to come across as a prat or anything but all I'm saying is he's out twice a day rain or shine. Ferdi is smart and he says he and Coppi are thinking →

Dear Hugo

→ about building their own team. Coppi is going to leave Bianchi and open a bike factory because he knows he can't keep going forever. He's been talking to a sponsor from Italy and the guy said he's a big fan of Ferdi so that's how it started. They've had a word and turns out they've loads of money and they don't know anythin about cycling! Ferdi reckons if they play their cards right they will clean up. Keep that under your hat pal because it's just between you and me. Even club riders have training diaries these days so you should think about one because it helps with the disc motivashernal side. I know you can't be doing with all that but it wouldn't be a bad idea to work out some sort of a plan now you're married pal? Besides what harm can a few long, steady winter rides do anyway? We can still Have a laugh even if we're married I reckon so my idea is why not skip a few track things and start coming out with us in the new year? The weight will come off much easier, you won't need to use the you-know-what and you'll be home with Sonja more. I honestly can't remember the last time we just went out for a bike ride together, and that's a shame pal!

F.

Zurigo. Il celebre corridore ciclista svizzero Hugo Koblet con la moglie, presso il caminetto della sua nuova casa, subito dopo il matrimonio. Prima di partire per il viaggio di nozze in Engadina, in Spagna e in Italia, Koblet e la moglie hanno fatto una breve sosta nella dimora destinata ad accoglierli al loro ritorno, fissato per la metà di gennaio, data di apertura della nuova stagione ciclistica. Hugo Koblet ha ventotto anni.

Zurigo. Koblet e la moglie nell'intimità della loro casa, un tipico e caratteristico interno svizzero. A sinistra la madre del corridore, a destra la madre della sposa nel costume locale. Com'è noto, Koblet si è unito in matrimonio il 6 dicembre scorso con la bellissima indossatrice ventitreenne Sonia Bühl, che lavora per le grandi sartorie zurighesi e parigine; Sonia ha dichiarato che probabilmente continuerà a fare il suo mestiere, così come Koblet farà il proprio. Si ritroveranno però, appena possibile, in questa casa modernissima e pure di aspetto patriarcale.

14.01.55

Guido Ceppi
photojournalism
Corso Galiera 4
Genova, 16142
Tel. 02. 231. 843

Hugo Koblet
Wassbergstrasse 206
Forch
Zurich Canton
Switzerland

Dear Mr Koblet,

I am Guido, the photographer who came to your lovely home for the Italian magazine. The editor told me your mother was unhappy with the choice of photos, so I thought I'd write and explain why we selected the ones we did.

As a freelance photojournalist, my job is to try to evoke whatever I find. I have to be faithful to the situation, and to interpret it as best I can through the photographs I make.

The morning we visited, we detected a slight unease between your wife, your mother and your mother-in-law. I assumed it was because you were recently married and they didn't really know one another, so it was understandable. It seemed like a classic newlywed scenario, where two completely different families are brought together. The photograph we used was an attempt to articulate that, and it was in no way my intention that your mother would find the images unflattering. I just wanted to produce a realistic representation of the moment, and that's why I chose the shot I did.

I do hope that helps to set your mind at rest.

Yours sincerely,
Guido Ceppi

Dear Hugo

28th June 2021

The 1952 Tour was supposed to have settled everything but it hadn't because Hugo hadn't even been there! It was all quite strange but I suppose I should mention that they'd both ridden the Giro. It doesn't really matter because it had been pointless. Hugo had been there to train, you see?. He'd wanted to be ready for the Tours of Switzerland and FRANnce, but for Fausto it had been different because was Italian which meant he was riding to win. Hugo lost 3 minutes in the first time trial, and then 8 in the big dolomite stage. IN THE final time trial he only lost 15 seconds to Fausto, and the difference was by then he'd ridden himself into condition. Fausto won the Giro and he was the campionissimo but I was still sure Hugo was the best and that he was preparing in the right way.

Now about that terrible thing at the Tour de Suisse because it's only right that I give my opinion. I remember that wew went to the start again but this time it was bateween the Giro and the Tour and that's why Coppi and Koblet had ben at different levels at the Giro. Fausto could rest after Giro and prepare for the Tour de France but Hugo couldn't so his way was to race all three. It was crazy even to try but he didn't think like the others and that was that. Hugo and Ferdi were the favourites as usual but then something happened to Hugo during the time trial down in Valais. The first 65 kilometres were on the valley road with just a few bumps here and there. He was leading as normal and it was going to be the day he won the race. I was listening on the radio and I'd calculated that if everything was normal he would take at least 3 minutes out of Ferdi and probably four. Then he started the climb up to the ski station and for some reason he collapsed. I think he lost 9 minutes or something, and we never understood why. They said he'd caught bronchitis because he'd done interviews after the stage in the Jura without changing out of his cycling clothes. That didn't seem to make sense though because surely if he'd caught bronchitis he wouldn't have been riding so well before the climb!! Anyway how someone like Hugo Koblet lose 9 minutes in 15 km to someone like Fornara? It didn't seem possible but it happened like that so it was.

He didn't brecover and that meant Fausto won the Tour as well. The least said about that the better because in my opinion it was most boring Tour de France ever. Without

Hugo there was nobody for Fausto to compete with you see? Kübler wasn't there either so our teeam didn't really have anyone AND THE others were just riding for stage wins & the podium. It was all a let-down and even Fausto looked bored in the last week.

....

29th June 2021

I promised myself I wouldn't do this after supper but I want to say something because people don't underatand. They see photogrpahs and read about the women and the comb and the money and the concl usion they make is that it was easy being Hugo Koblet. Well I was following him closer than anyone and my opinion isn't that one because after 1951 something always seemed to go wrong for Hugo when he rode the Giro and the Tour. Something bad happened betzween him and Coppi at the 1953 Giro but I didn't understand what. They fell out when Fausto took the jersey and the thing about that is that Hugo had never fallen out with anyone before in his life! They say Coppi tricked him out of the maglia rosa and it's possible. Hugo was very angry and I'd never know him like that before. When they asked him he just said it was something personal between them and nobody else's business.It wasn't like him to respond like that because he never lostz his temper and he was never normally impolite.

    Everyone knows abouit the crash at the Tour. He'd always been a daredevil descender but he was heavier now and they don't recover as well do they?. (You see the the more he struggled on the climbs the more risks he had to take on the descents?)

    I will never forget my dad telling me what had happened when I got home that day. It made me sick to my stomach, especially after he'd lost the Giro like that. I had to sit down and I responded badly to my mother. She didn't say anything at first but then after a few minutes she said, "Why don't you two go to the park for a bit of fresh air?". That was a strange thing for her to say but as we were walking along my dad explained that it was only sport and I shouldn't forget it. I didn't really understand what he was getting at but I decided it must have been important because he wouldn't have made me go to the park with him otherwise. (I iunderstand now of course and he was right.)

Dear Hugo

Anyway as we were walking home I told my dad that Koblet would win next year, but the fact is I was wrong. He didn't win again, and he didn't even reach Paris again.

29th June 2021

Now I want to explain why I've always maintained he was thegreatest. People who never saw him think I'm crazy because he only rode three Tours de France and he only finished one. I understand that but when I say he was the greatest I don't mean he was the best. They say he ate too much and they were right. They say he wasn't smart enough and they were right. They say that if he'd trained like Kübler he''d have won the Tour three or four times and they're probably right because Coppi was getting towards the end and the fact is that Bobet wasn't in his class. They're all right but I don't care because I'm right as well. What I mean by that is that if he'd done all those things and been all those things he wouldn't have been Hugo Koblet!

Everyone knew that Kübler was more '"serious'. He'd grown up in a poor family out and through cycling he could drag himself up and prove that he was was aa winner. The fact is that nobody trained harder, except maybe Magni because he was a maniac as well. Ferdi always looked like he was suffering terribly when he was riding and the more he suffered the more people liked it. With HHugo it was different because he made cycling look easy. THAT Was probably why a lot of Swiss people identiffied more with Ferdi but my dad explained that it was part of the show. It was one of the ways he had of promoting himself and that was part of the show. I suippose it was a bit like Hugo with the comb and the eau de cologne – he didn't really need to do it but professional cyclists back then had to create an image and it worked. Anyway I suppose Ferdi won the Tour before Hugo and that big nose of his was a gift from god because everyone in Switzerland knew him. They called him "2Ferdi the Nose".

What Ferdi didn't have (in my opinion at least9) was Hugo's magic. Koblet was more than a cyclist, you see? He rode a bike but for me he was a poet, or a sort of artist. He wasn't interested in his career in the way Ferdi was, and he didn't feel like he had anything to prove. I suppose I mean that cycling was freedom for him, not toil like for Ferdi. He couldn't plan anything or organize anything so he just got up each day and followed his instincts. Each day was different for him and I think every day was an adventure.. I think he was a dreamer and I mean that in a good way. He couldn't go out and train on the same roads every day because it would have driven him crazy. He always needed to go somewhere and to do something and he needed to experience new things.

There's something else I have to say about K&K before I stop and it's this:- People talked about Ferdi the fighter but in his own way Hugo was fighting as well. What I mean is that he was always good to people and he tried not to be contaminated by the way they behaved with him. For example he would never have done whatever Coppi did at the Giro, or behaved the way Ferdi and Bartali did with money. I think things like that would have destroyed something inside someone like him because he wasn't capabale of playing those tricks . I have a theory that was why he liked riding the track so much. It was much less calculating and more impulsive. It was purer and there were less tricks, and he was more able to just be himself.

1st July 2021

Today I want to start by giving my opinion about Clerici and the 1954 Giro. This is because I think it's an important thing for anyone who is serious about trying to understand Koblet..

He wasn't a champion, Clerici, but he was a good rider and he won the Giro y half an hour. Hugo rode for him as a domestique and that had bever ghappened before. What I mean is that teams were very small and the great champions didn't do that sort of thing back then

To be honest the Italians couldn't understand what was happening but I think I know and this sis wahat I think:-

The Italians had never fought fair with Hugo and I've already explained that he wouldnt have understood it. He would never say anything but letting Clerici go with that break was his way to made them pay. Clerici had only taken Swiss nationality because they'd treated him badly the previous year and they wouldn't have treated him like that if he hadn't been brought up in Zurich. Clerici was italian, but they didn't think of him as a "2real italain" you see? They'd threw him out of the race and his team had sacked him on the spot, and all because he'd helped Hugo. The thing about that is that helping other people was natural for Clerici because he'd grown up in Switzerland and thats how we do things here. It didn't matter that Hugo was riding for a different team because we're taught that everyone has to help everyone elsem. Clerici had been punished for being a good sport and that was why he'd renounced his Italian citizenship and become Swiss.

What Im trying to say is that Coppi would never have allowed one of his gregarrios to win because it would have been bad for Bianchi's business2 if a nobody had won the Giro. Magni and BARtali wouldn't allow something like that either. They had to protect their interests so they were jealous of each other and jealous of the others. Hugo wasn't like that at all because he wasn't like other cyclists. He was happy for diffrent people to win and he didn't understand why they weren't.

He wasn't as good as he'd been before but he was still probably the best rider at that Giro. Clerici was his friend though and I think in some way he preferred to finish 2 nd. It made a kind of justice and I strongly believe that Coppi understood that as well. Whatever he'd done the previous year had upset Koblet so when Clerici won it helped to square everything up between them. Even though they both lost (Coppi and Koblet I mean) they both won as well and that was because of Hugo. He helped Coppi to clear his conscoiunce and after that they became friends again. He also learned the Italians a lesson in sportsmanship and good behaviour. I hope it's clear and you get my meaning because only Koblet would and could have done something like that.

. k&k K&K agreed to ride the 1954 Tour together together and that was a very big thing for Swiss cycling. Bit by bit they were learning to live sid-by-side and they almost became a sort of 'partnership'. My mum always said rrespect was one of the most important things and dad said it made sense for them to get along as well. By behaving correctly they became more popular and the more popular they were the more they money they earned. I hadn't really thought about that but it was a very Swiss way of thinking. Ours isn't really a natrual country (it's a confederation, not a normal country). We have different lanmguages, cultures and religions but we get along because we have patience and we always try to obey the rules and to be correct. Anyway people were fascinnated by the K&K ANd when they saw them getting on together it made them feel good. We were looking forward to it but it worked out terrible FOR me as a kOBLETIST. i I was sure Hugo was going to win and it seemed like even the French wanted him to win. They loved him because of how he was and because he'd had a lot of bad luck. Anyway he was a few seconds behind Bobet when they got to the Pyrenees and the others were out of it. What happened was that the weather was terrible, all misty and dark like it sometimes is down there. He was on the descent of the Aubisque but he couldn'r see so it was another terrible crash. He started the next day but he lost 25 minutes and then he had to abandon. Kübler did aa good tour but I had difficulty about it because I knew that Hugo was suffering. I told my dad I was sure he wouldn't be going back to the Tour5 because it had caused him too much pain. My dad said something like "the luck's not on his side is it son?".

....

2nd July 2021

The finaal stage of the 1955 Tour de Suisse was a time trial and it finished at the track at Oerlikon. My dad had been off work for a week or so because he hadn't been feeling well. It was a nice day with a lovely breeze though and that's why he told my mum he was going with me whether she liked itor not. Mum told him he was being an idiot but looking back I don't think he was an idiot at all. i think he knew it was serious and that it would be the last day we'd spend to gether at the cycling.

    I think they made the route so that the climbs were further than normal from the stage finishes. That way Hugo would be able to get back on because he was the best descender (when he didn't falloff) and the time trial would be the deciding element. It was a deliberate thing because they knew his road career was finishing and they wanted him to win a third Tour de Suisse to be equal with Ferdi. When Hugo came past with the bouquet and the yellow jersey, dad just smiled and winked at me, and I smiled and winked back. We didn't say anything because there was no need to. We both understood what was happening and dad knew I was happy being theree at the end of it. My being happy made my dad happy, you see? If I'd known we provably wouldn't have gone, but he said it was just a chest infection.

    I'm going to call it a night now sory.

Dear Hugo

22.01.55
MAERTENS & FINK
LEGAL ASSOCIATES
ANTWERPERWEG 44,
90452, ROTTERDAM
TEL: 22.965.98

Hugo Koblet
Wassbergstrasse 206
CH-8127
Forch
Zurich
Switzerland

Dear Mr. Koblet,

We act as legal counsel for Mr Henk Groenendijk.

In quality of promoter/organizer of the "Night of the Stars" cycling event at Rotterdam Sports Palais on 28 January, Mr Groenendijk informs us that you now claim you are unable to appear because you have a prior engagement.

We remind you of the binding contract you signed on 16 December (copy enclosed). We also remind you that your name has appeared extensively in advance publicity, on the official programme (copy enclosed) and on advertising materials posted around Rotterdam.

Our client is a man of excellent standing locally, and has acted in good faith at all times. Failure on your part to appear will damage his reputation gravely, and disadvantage him financially. In that case, be aware that we will have no option but to pursue a substantive claim against you for compensation.

Yours,
Maertens & Fink.
cc. H. Groenendijk

02.08.55
BUCHMANN BROS.
NOTARY AND
CONVEYANCING
SERVICES
Thalstrase 7, 8032,
Kloten, Zurich
TEL: +41 44 774 982

Mr & Mrs H Koblet
Wassbergstrasse 206
8127
Forch
Zurich

Dear Mr & Mrs Koblet,

Re: Sternen Restaurant, Dorfstrasse 22, 8302 Kloten

We act on behalf of Widmar Associates, commercial agents for the sale of the Sternen Restaurant in Kloten. The purchaser, Mr Adolf Koblet, informs us that you will remit the 25 per cent deposit to facilitate the assignation of the lease. Further, Mr Koblet informs us that, upon completion, you will act as financial guarantors for the balance.

Please contact me at your earliest convenience in order that we may move the matter forward.

Yours sincerely,
Emil Buchmann

04.10.55
Fausto Coppi
Novi Ligure

Dear Hugo,

Everything is arranged for me. The team will be Carpano-Coppi and Ferdi will do the Italian races with us. He and I will be the old ones!

```
MOREAU FINE ARTS
Pfalzgasse 33, 8001 Zurich
Tel:775521
COMPANY REG:776318 VAT: 204987ZU



Invoice. 164

6 October 1955

Mr & Mrs H Koblet
Wassbergstrasse 206
8127
Forch


To:

Varlin "Lakeside"          CHF 17.000

Picasso "Abstract face"    CHF 31,000

VAT                        CHF 3,040


TOTAL PAYABLE              CHF 51,040
```

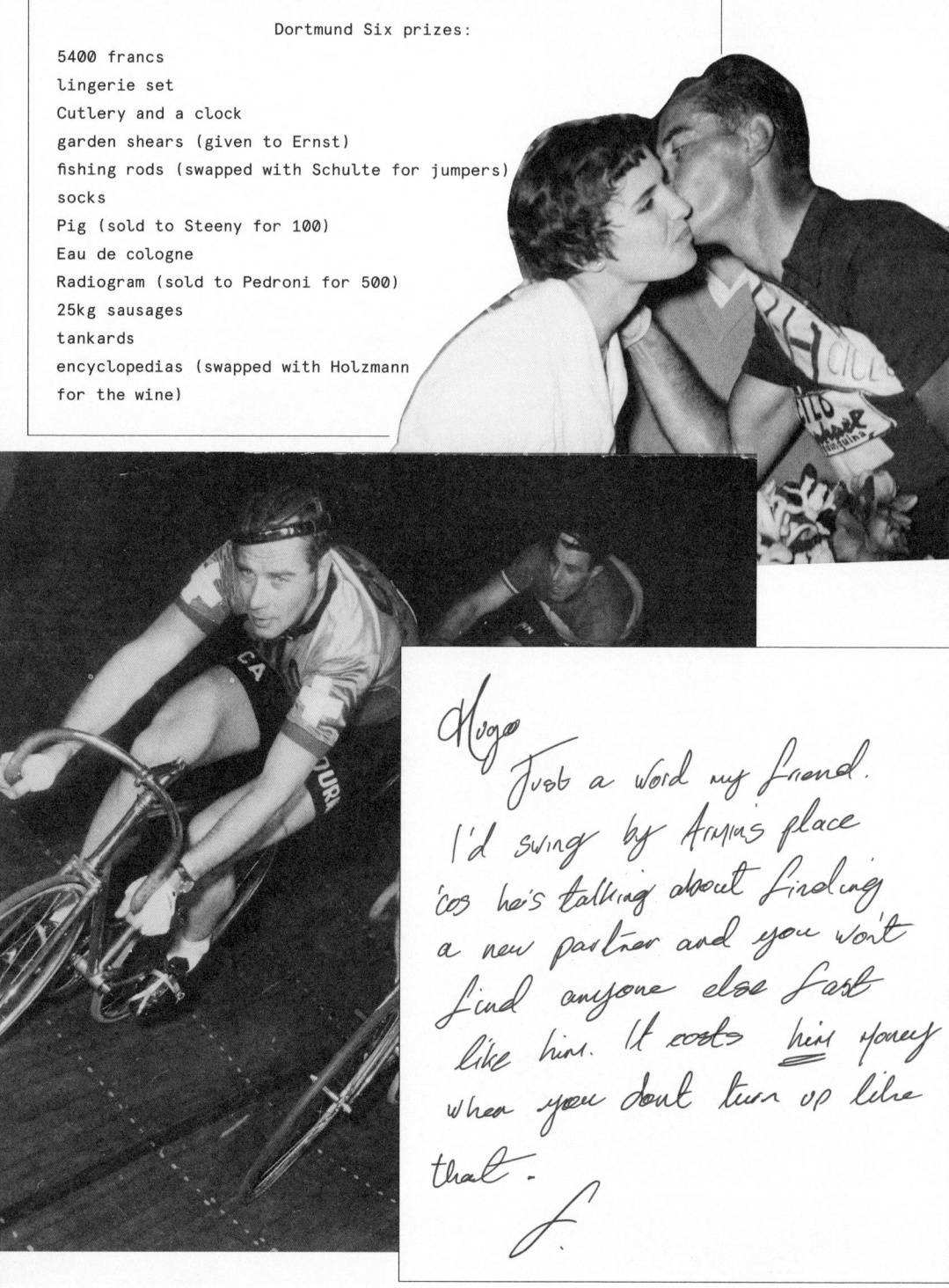

```
Dortmund Six prizes:
5400 francs
lingerie set
Cutlery and a clock
garden shears (given to Ernst)
fishing rods (swapped with Schulte for jumpers)
socks
Pig (sold to Steeny for 100)
Eau de cologne
Radiogram (sold to Pedroni for 500)
25kg sausages
tankards
encyclopedias (swapped with Holzmann
for the wine)
```

Hugo
Just a word my friend.
I'd swing by Armin's place
'cos he's talking about finding
a new partner and you won't
find anyone else fast
like him. It costs him money
when you don't turn up like
that.

Tragella says N Bianchi want you to take my place and Belloni wants you as well. They will pay double what Learco gives you, no problem, and you can do all the track you want. I think you should accept with Bianchi because there won't be any problems. Learco always says you are like a son for him but he pays you like a farm hand!

Little Faustino is doing well now – I have trouble to keep up with his rythyms. Maybe you and Sonja next? The world needs a Kobletino!

F.

11.10.55
Fausto Coppi
Novi Ligure

Dear friend,
Think about it because if you won't do the Tour anymore there will be no criteriums. You always need cash and it doesn't matter if you win or not. It doesn't matter about Learco either – cycling is bussiness for him and he will understand! You are 31 0 now and you weigh 85 kilos. Time is running fast. Take the money!

Fausto.

22.11.55
Fausto Coppi
Novi Ligure

Dearest Hugo,
So you will stay with Learco - you are a good man Hugo and i think sometimes too good. I respect your loyalty but dometimes in this life you have to p ut your own interests first. You have to learn to say no.

All fine - see you in Paris.

Fausto.

06.01.56

Obergass 3,
Eglisau. Tel: 841

Hugo Koblet
Wassbergstrasse 206
8127
Forch
Zurich

Dearest Hugo,
First and foremost, we at Vivi-Kola would like to wish you a happy and prosperous new year.

Time rolls on for all of us, and the soft drinks world never stands still. As such we've been renewing our marketing activities, and have decided to diversify somewhat. In light of your reduced activity we won't be renewing our partnership, but we'd like to thank you for the important contribution you've made these past five years.

Yours sincerely
Emile Reinle

Dear Hugo

```
02.03.56
Hallenstadion
Velodrome
Wallisellenstrasse
45, 8050, Zurich

Hugo Koblet
Wassbergstrasse 206
Forch
8127
Zurich
```

Dear Hugo,

I'm most delighted you will ride the Six with Ferdi. We'll have another great success, with still more prizes. I'm told that last year they sold 16,000 bottles of beer. With you and Ferdi we'll be sure to sell out every night, so who knows?

    Best for now.

```
15.03.56
MOREAU FINE ARTS
Pfalzgasse 33, 8001
Zurich
Tel: 775521
COMPANY REG: 776318
VAT: 204987ZU

Mr & Mrs H Koblet
Wassbergstrasse 206
Forch
```

Dearest Hugo and Sonja,

I forgot to mention that a small balance of 10.000 Francs is still outstanding for the two oils. I expect this is just an oversight on your part, what with you flying here, there and everywhere in your glamorous lives! Call me when you have a moment, and we can arrange to meet at the gallery. We are currently showcasing an exciting young figurative painter from Lucerne. His name is Lasalle, and I feel sure his work will appeal to you greatly.

    Kind regards,
    Elizabeth

KOBLET HUGO!!

no tour d france no tour suisse allways excuses!! velta espangja DNF paris to roubeis DNF! poor KOBLET!! team not good bike not good feet no good form training KOBLET!! work
    angina all what stopped me bastard WHAT was it like KOBLET! 5th at Wohlen spiked the bidon they didcome over light headed me went over thre with the brother I did squared him up good and propper light headed he was then KOBLET!! all fancy friends now race car fast driving skiing for famous ones is dangerous that KOBLET? raclette chocolate schampeyne where it stop is what i ask KOBLET! YOU prancing about wearing you shandy-pants. THINK ON!,

Chopard.

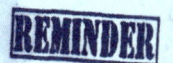

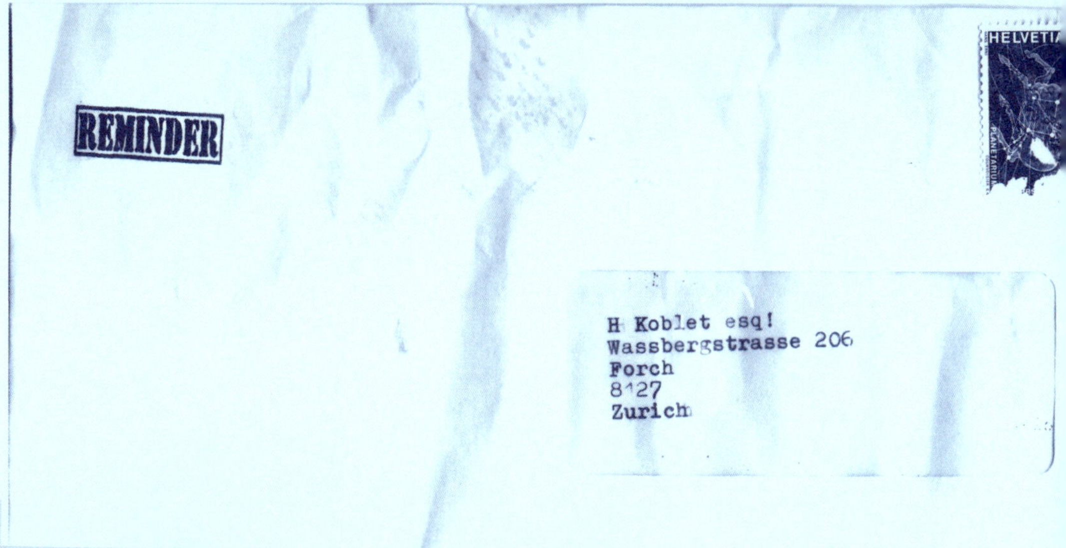
REMINDER
HELVETIA
H Koblet esq!
Wassbergstrasse 206
Forch
8127
Zurich

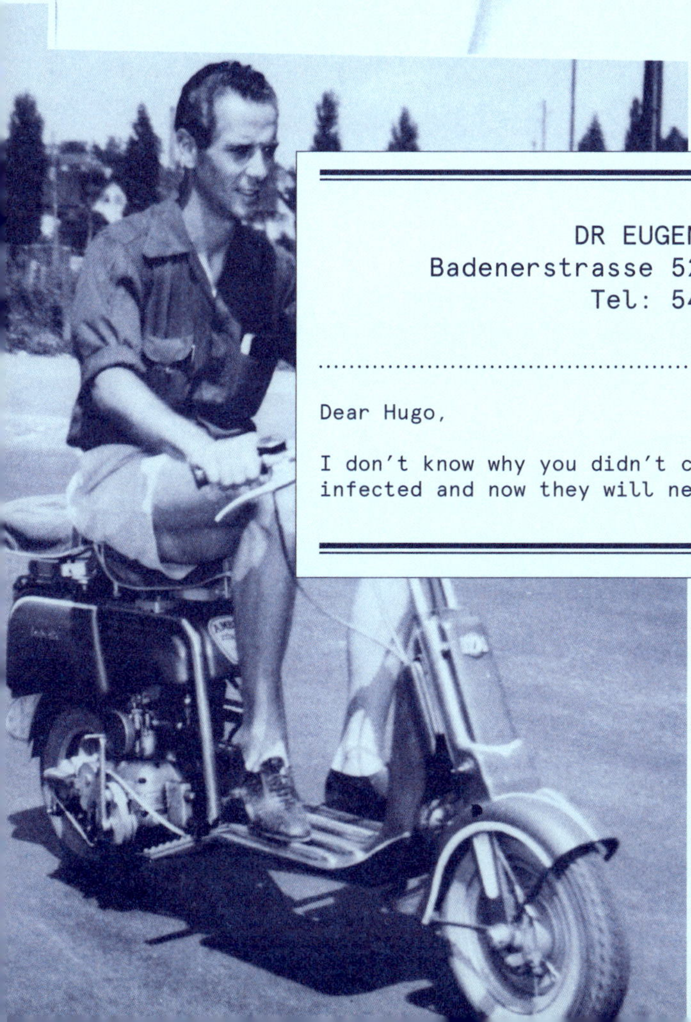

DR EUGEN RUFT
Badenerstrasse 526, Zurich 8004
Tel: 549.90

Dear Hugo,

I don't know why you didn't come sooner but it's infected and now they will need to operate.

1957 road races
- Settimana Sarda
- Milano–Torino
- Milano–Sanremo
- Flanders
- Paris–Roubaix
- G P Ciclomotoristico
- Romandie
- Giro
- Td. Suisse
- Nationale

DUOMO DI MILANO

It's because every time I get home she's sat there, in my new house, smoking and reading her trashy novels. I thought I was marrying you, not your mother! I'll arrive at the station on Wednesday morning. Assuming you can drag yourself away from your card game, pick me up at 11.30 and DON'T BRING HER WITH YOU!

TO: Hugo Koblet
Wassbergstrasse
206 8127
Forch
Zurich

Dear Götti and auntie Sonja, Thank you for having me at your house at christmas. I had a great time and really enjoyed making cookies,
x x

Daniel DROUSSET
3, Avenue Armand
Guillebaud, Antony
(Seine),
Tel: 05-044

Dear Mrs Koblet,

If I've understood correctly, you're suggesting I owe your husband money from the 1951 criteriums? I'm sorry but if he failed to collect his winnings that's his problem not mine! Years have passed and I can't just send 25,000 francs! It's not my fault if he didn't have a bank account. Warm regards to him anyway. Does he know you wrote to me?

Drousset

29.10.56

Stroppa AG, Corso
San Gottardo 1,
6380, Chiasso
Tel: (091) 21895

Hugo Koblet
Wassbergstrasse 206
8127
Forch
Zurich

Dear Mr Koblet,

I confirm that Moto Parilla will collect the motorcycle on 6 November at 11 o'clock. Please ensure the registration book is at hand.

Your sincerely,

Ciro Stroppa (Managing Director)

28.01.57
Gerd Schaffner
Consultant
Obstetrician-
Gynecologist
Bachmattweg
414,5000, Aarau
Tel: (056) 4310

Mr & Mrs H Koblet
Wassbergstrasse 206
8127
Forch
Zurich

Dear Mr & Mrs Koblet,

If, as seems likely, the womb and ovaries are healthy, I suggest you proceed as follows:

   1. Regular intercourse
   2. Increased sexual activity immediately before and during ovulation
   3. Maintain a high-iron diet
   4. Avoid stressful situations and intense exercises

If nothing of consequence happens within, say, six months, feel free to contact me once more.
Yours sincerely,
Schaffner

Dear Hugo

```
                                                    MOD: 19844/57A
                                                       RADIOTELEGRAM
       DESTINATION: KOBLET, GP MOTOCLISTICO ROCCARASO/CAMPOBASSO IT
                 ISSUEr: DR JULEN SAINT THEODUL CLINIC ZERMATT
                      ZERmSND1ZURICH-SD790832. 26 APR 15.01
                                                         WORDS: 30
```

MRS KOBLET FELL while SKIING AT GORNERGRAT STOP
LEG FRACTURES+SEVERE BRUISING = OPERATION
REQUIRED STOP NO HEAD INJURY + NO THREAT TO LIFE
COME ASAP STOP TEL 027 779662 JULEN STOP

```
Daniel DROUSSET
3, Avenue Armand
Guillebaud, Antony
(Seine), Tel: 05-
044
```

Dear Hugo,

Sorry you won't ride the Giro. The Italians look after their own and Guerra is Guerra. A new career as a derny driver? Are you sure? Speak with Wambst and he will help!.
 If you want some criteriums after the Tour, no problem. I can arrange madisons at Vel D'Hiv as well. The money won't be like before, but come on Tuesday and we can try to do something.

Un abraccio!

```
AUGUSTE WAMBST
Rue des Vosges 22
88400
Gérardmer
```

Dear friend,

I hope your lady is recovering. I understand your situation and I will come - meet we at the station at 13.30. You are tall and quite big, so you can be good for a stayer driver. I will teach you and if Drousset helps with the organizers we can do something. Don't worry about the other thing – we will speak about it.

Auguste

06.07.57
PEOPLE'S BANK OF
ZURICH
Registered office:
Paradeplatz 9b,
8010, Zurich

Hugo Koblet
Wassbergstrasse 206
8127
Forch
Zurich

Dear Mr Koblet,

In accordance with bank policy, I write with regards to the increased level of activity in your account. Should you wish to explore how best to manage your arrangements, I am happy so to do. My direct line is 88429, and you may call me at any time.

Yours sincerely,

Herbert Lubbet, manager.

09.10.57
Lehmann & Frei
Attorneys AG
Grundtsrasse 4
Winterthur
8400
COMPANY REG:125513
VAT: 10986WI

Mr & Mrs H Koblet
Hotzestrasse 11
Rietholz 8112
Oetelfingen
Zurich

Dear Mr & Mrs Koblet,

We act on behalf of Kaltz Food Services Ltd, whose registered office is in Zelweg, Winterthur. Our client is a creditor of the Sternen Restaurant in Kloten. The proprietor is one Adolf Koblet, and we note that you act as guarantors.

Despite the repeated efforts of our client, the proprietor has failed to remit payment for a number of invoices, dating back to October 1956. The total outstanding is 11,241 francs (statement enclosed herewith) and an order of foreclosure is now pending. I am legally obliged to inform you that, in the event that the business is declared insolvent, your legal obligations as guarantors will remain unaltered.

The insolvency order may be avoided if full settlement is received within 14 days, or if a viable payment plan can be mutually agreed between the two parties. Failure to accomplish either will result in enforced closure of the business, whereupon both yourselves and the proprietor will be summonsed to appear before the magistrature.

Yours sincerely,

Siegfied Heinze (associate partner)

Dear Hugo

28.11.57
Fausto Coppi
Novi Ligure

Dearest Hugo,

I have spoken to Luis Frigerio. All seems good! They have accepted so and Oscar Hernandez will be our agent. He is helping me and he will arrange every thing. There will be a "series" of races, I think pursuits and Mdisons. Looks like we will proably be there all of February. We will start in Colombia, then Mexico and Venezuela.

    I will go in December and stay for Christmas. I'll probably retire down there. I might buy a bike factory – why not? Come for Christmas if you want. They say the Colombians are very good !! We can prepare together.

Fausto.

```
                                    MODULE UNIVERSAL
                                     TELEGRAM OFFICE
            SENDING STATION: bogota 16b996f4/frigerio l
            RECEIVING STATION: mexico city mexico mx0452
            DESTINATION: koblet/coppi hotel palisandro
                    colonia centrale san miguel mexico .
                            Time/date: 15.37/07-02-58
                                           Words: 14
```

CHEQUE BOUNCED. ACCOUNT CLOSED. HERNANDEZ VANISHED. POLICE NOT HELPING. $7200 – WHAT TO DO?

L

19.05.58
HEINZE, ROTH & THALMANN
LAND AGENTS
ALTE LANDSTRASSE 4,
8700, KÜSNACHT.
TEL: 66.983

Mr & Mrs H Koblet
Wassbergstrasse 206
8127
Zurich

Re: Formal offer: Wassbergstrasse 206, Forch.

Dear Mr & Mrs Koblet,

I confirm that we are in receipt of a written offer for the house. It's some way below the asking price, but Mr Manz is able to proceed with immediate effect. I enclose a copy, and look forward to hearing from you in due course.
Yours sincerely,
Konrad Roth

```
MODULE 5/12-1958 v
TELEGRAM OFFICE
DESTINATION: koblet-oetelfingen-Switzerland.
ISSUED BY: milano01b
Milanoml55409-zurichzu77/12. 30.05.1958.10.12
Words: 16
```

SEEMS LIKE YOU ARE IN A TIGHT SPOT. WILL SEE WHAT I CAN DO. SORRY TO HEAR ABOUT YOUR MOTHER

E

21.06.58

Enrico Mattei
Via Sebastopoli 88,
20196, Milano

Mr H Koblet
Hotzestrasse 11
Rietholz 8112
Oetelfingen
Zurich

Dear Hugo,

First and foremost, many thanks for the jersey; it will appear very elegant here in my office.

I've given the situation some considerable thought, and I think a solution may be at hand.

The company is assuming responsibility for marketing and distribution of Italian automotive brands in Venezuela. These are to include FIAT and Alfa Romeo, and in all probability Pirelli as well. We have made significant investments there, and with the discovery of oil the economy has been enjoying significant growth. They are building a very impressive new transport infrastructure, and our objective is to capitalize by establishing a network of dealers.

I believe this represents an excellent opportunity both for you and for ourselves. By promoting European sophistication, design and quality, we aim to rival the mass-market American manufacturers. By focusing on excellence as distinct to price, we will attract a more discerning clientele.

My offer to you is that of an "ambassadorial" position, but a full-time one. You are well-known down there, and your fame, influence and contacts will help "sell" the idea of Italian motoring into the Venezuelan business community. Bombieri and his team will assist, but once you hit your stride, you should be eminently capable of making inroads.

Dear Hugo

Be aware that neither English nor French are widely spoken, even within the business community. You will therefore need to develop your Spanish quickly, but that didn't ought to be difficult given the excellence of your Italian. Once your Spanish is order you will start attending "high society" events, and for this we will provide a suitable Alfa Romeo. It will provide a talking point, and from there you will create a network of contacts amongst prominent politicians and influential individuals.

As regards accommodation, we have optioned a beautiful apartment in the Edifico Galopin, the most futuristic and luxurious skyscraper in Caracas. Flights to New York are plentiful, so Sonja will have no difficulty if she intends to work for an agency there. Given the nature of your work, we envisage an initial three-year tenure beginning in Novmber. We shall devise a suitable remuneration package, performance-based so as to better reward your endeavors.

Assuming this is acceptable in principle, we should aim to meet as soon as is mutually convenient. If you are agreeable, we could look towards the afternoon of Wednesday 9 here in Milan. Please confirm by return.

Yours sincerely,

E.M
Enrico Mattei

22.09.58

Latin America HQ
Headquarters: NW
36th Street, Miami
33142

Mr & Mrs Koblet
Hotzestrasse 11
Rietholz 8112
Oetelfingen
Zurich
Switzerland

Dear Mr and Mrs Koblet,

Please find enclosed your tickets (business class) to Caracas, Venezuela, via New York City.

Your itinerary is as follows:

11 Nov: Dep: Kloten Zurich	08.40 GMT+1	
Arr: LaGuardia New York	17.50 EDT	
Dep: LaGuardia New York	20.15 EDT	
Arr: Maiquetìa Caracas	05.30 VET	

Please be sure to arrive at your airport of origin two hours in advance of the scheduled flight time.

Best regards.

THE HERLANDER HOSPICE
CARE · SUPPORT · COMPASSION

Gerbeweg 19, 8708, Männedorf. Tel: 079 66 12 08

2 October 1958

Mr H Koblet
Hotzestrasse 11
Rietholz 8112
Oetelfingen
Zurich

Dear Mr Koblet,

Re: Helene Koblet-Gross

Your brother, Mr. Adolph Koblet, informs me that you are administering your mother's care. As such, please find attached our statement of account to month ending September.

Please remit by return.

Yours sincerely,
Otto Franck

09.10.58
Hallenstadion
Velodrome
Wallisellenstrasse
45, 8050, Zurich

Hugo Koblet
Hotzestrasse 11
Rietholz 8112
Oetelfingen
Zurich

Dearest Hugo,

It's difficult for me to write this, but write it I must. The loss of Emil is a shock to us all, for he's been the heart and soul of Swiss track cycling for as long as anyone can remember. However, as we approach your farewell I know he would want me to thank you for the limitless pleasure you have provided, and for the way you've conducted yourself throughout.

    Seemingly all good things must end so it's right that you're stopping now just as it's right that Ferdi is stopping. 1954 suddenly feels like a very long time ago but nobody will forget the joy of seeing the two of you riding our inaugural Six-Day together. This place was wonderful back then thanks to you.

    Everything is prepared for Friday next. Obviously ticket sales aren't what they were, but we're hopeful we'll get 5000 or so to see you on your way. We start at 20.15 and you'll be paired with Schulte. You will need to be here no later than 17.00 beccause there will be quite a lot to get through.

Ernst

Dear Hugo

3rd July 2021

I still followed cycling, but not as closely as I had before. Life was different andI wasn't a teenager anymore after all. Things were changing all the time, and I semed to be running to eep up.

    The other thing was that I'd always followed cycling with my dad. Without him it wasn't nearly as interedting and of course the K&K time was passed. There was a new group of riders in Switzerland but they weren't as good and they never won any of the big races in France, Italy or Belhgium. Graf was good at time trials but the rest were just average riders . When they never win you're just waiting for something to happen all the time.

    I carried on riding my bike (I didn't stop riding it until 10 years ago but that's anotherstory) but I didn't renew my racing license. The lads at the club weren't happy but I didn't have time because I was a working man and I had a lot of responsibilities. The word I would use TO dscribe my cycling would be leisurely. What i mean is that sometimes on a Sunday morning i'd ride along the lakeside for acouple of hours. I couldn't go very fast because I wasn't fit, , but after a while it didn't bother me anymore. I decided I'd have time to train properly later when I was settled down with my wife and family. For now though I was just happy to enjoy the peace and quiet. From time to time I'd bump into someone I knew but most of them were doing serious training and I wasn't. I always kept my bike in good order even though it wasn't the most up to date. My grandson has the Cilo now and he keeps it really well. I tought him that a well-looked after old bike is faster than a neglected new one.

    ~~I forgot to~~

4th July 2021

I was going to say that I was the main breadwinner in the family now. My dad had explained everything to me before he went and we'd agreed thatI had to take care of my mum. That meant working as hard as a I could and the mopre I worked the better it was, and I'd given my dad my word that I would do that as best I could. My sister she started in the secretarial pool of a bank but she was only at the beginning so it didn't pay much. Mymum she got a patrt-time job at the butcher's and that helped. It was good for her because it was a way to be with people and to get through the days. It was good for me and my sister as well. What I mean is that we could see that slowly she was getting used to her new life and the people there knew our situation. Mum been going there for years you see?

I did as much overtime as mr K would let me. He was a good man and he awlays made sure there was plenty of work. We seemed to do a lot of removals, house-clearances and things like that so he and I spent a lot of time together. If we went out on a styaturday morning I earned extra money. Mr K wasn't rich and it was only a few francs extra but it helped a lot and mr K said he liked working on Saturday mornings. He said it didn't really feel like work because it was just me and him in the van and there was less pressure. I think he liked the company and he liked moving things and being involved. It was his business but during the week he was

mainly in the office doing paperwork and organizing. He was concerned about my wellness and I could tell he liked my mum even though he wasn't the type to just come out and say it. He was a bit awkward like that you see:- a bit shy. On Saturdays he'd pick me up and then drop me again, and my sister must have noticed because one day she told my mum she should try to be friends with him andmaybe go for a walk or something. Mum said blushed and she said she didn't have time for any of that nonsense. Shesaid she'd more than enough to be getting on with thankyou very much! Do'nt get me wromg because mr K wasn't trying to replace my dad or anything like that. I think it was jus that he didn't have a family of his own and he had no brothers or sistsres either.

What happened was that I heard an inter-view with Koblet on the radio. They said he was stopping and he admitted that he was worn out. He said he'd made too many mistakes but it was what it was and he was going to make a new life Venezuela. It was to do with selling Italian cars or oil or something. He said there was going to be one last Madison at the Hallenstadion on Friday to celebrat him, and everyone in cycling was going to be there including Kübler. I decided I had to be there as well.

i I decided I didn't want to go with the lads from the club. I'd drifted apart from them and they wouldn't have understood anyway. They would have wanted to drink beer and clown around and I wasnï't interested in that. So I decided it would be best if I just went on my own because that way it would just be me, my dad and Hugo again. The idea was that and we'd say goodbye to Hugo and in some way he'd say goodbye to me and dad.it was probably silly but that was my idea anyway.

 When we were having supper my mum said she'd heard about Koblet from a guy at thew shop who'd known dad. She asked what I thought and I said I'd made up my mind to go. When I told her I was going on my own she put her foot down and sai 'oh no you're not!' She said he would have wanted that we all went together and she meant my dad, not Hufgo. My sister she wanted to come as well, and I was surprised by that because she had her friends and we hardly ever went anywhere together. I told her not to be stupid but then she reminded me of the train ride to my auntie's that morning and said I didn't have a choice. When she said that it made me realize that my dad would have wanted it that way. I hadn't really wanted to go on my own anyway if im being honest. I'd promised I'd take care of my mum and sister but now I understood that they were trying to take care of me and I hadn't really thought of it like that before.

....

5th July 2021

We were on the sixth or seventh row and we were right in the middle of the track. I'd been in that place lots of times so I knew where to go you see? At the same itime I was with my mum and sister and I ADMIT THAT I WASn't sure how to behave so I started explaining cycling things to my mum and sister. I started with how a Madison works, who the strongest riders were and what the tactics would be. At first they pretended to be interested but after a while I could tell they were communicating in some sort of silent code. When I asked what the problem was my sister she started laughing at me. She said 'Stop going on will you? You hardkly ever say anything at home and we couldn't care less who wins as long as we're together!" What she was I was taking it all much too seriously and foregetting that we were supposed to be enjoying ourselves. Anyway after that it was much better because I calmed down and we had fun so that made it feel a bit likie dad was there with us in some way. We talked about him so it was like being in the living room at home but like being in the stafdium at the same time if you see what I mean. They didn't need me spelling the cycling out to them because they weren't stupid after all.

When the last warm-up race was on my sister said she fancied a lemonade and I said I'd go with her and get a bottle of beer while I was there. Mum said she'd like a beer as well and that was when me and my sister we just looked at each other with our mouths open! we couldn't believe it you see and my sister went, 'MOTHER! BEER? MY GOODNESS!'

So we went down into the concourse me and my sister, and when we got to the front of the queue she went 'Elke! I didn't know you worked here as well!'

The girl who was serving behind the bar worked with my sister in the typing pool you see? She said her dad was on the cycling committee so she was always there helping because she had no choice in the matter. My sister told her about my dad and why we were there. Elke sttarted getting the drinks and she told me that without my sister making her laugh she'd go nuts in that place with all those boring, serious old ones. She said her dad never stopped going on about cycling and he'd been upset because Keller had died and now Koblet was stopping. Then my sister introduced her to me a bit more correctly. We chatted for a couple of minutes before the race finished and the concourse started filling up with people wanting beer. Elke said 'it was very nice meting you' to me and I said it was very nice meeting her aa well. My sister started laughing at me again then.

....

6th July 2021

Hugo and Schulte didn't win the race (well they were too old) and afterwards there were speaches and things . All sorts of people came up and gave Hugo awards, flowers and suchlike. The guy from Cilo gave him a special gold watch and thanked him everything he'd done for cycling. The last to come up was Kübler and that was when my sister had to give my mum her handkerchief.

The thing I most remember is Hugo's face. I hadn't seen him close up since that last afternoon with my dad and 3 years had passed. Now he looked much older - almost like he was the same age as my dad when he'd died.

The following morning I was out in the van with mr K, thinking about erything that had happened. He must

Dear Hugo

have noticed something was wrong because he asked me if something wasn't right. I told him about my mum when they did the speeches and about meeting Elke. He said I could go home if I didn't feel up to it but I said I didn't want to because I wasn't sick or anything like that.
I explained that it had been lovely to be there with my mum and mysister and that it felt like a chapter of my life was ending. I said that with my dad and Koblet and everything it was probably all just a bit too much for me to take in and that was probably why I'd been so tongue-tied with Elke.

   I said it was just a feeling but as we were talking about it I started to understand a bit more. I think that what was wrong with me was that I was a bit worried about Koblet. Mr K he asked what I meant and I said I didn't know how to explain but after the race had finished he'd looked completely different. He said he was probably just tired after the Madison but it wasn't that because I knew him. I SAID IT WAS probably because he'd always been a kind of super hero for me and now I understood that it wasn't like that. There was more in life than cycling and he was just a normal person like the rest of us. When they'd asked him what he was going to do next he'd seemed unsure and in some way a bit lost. Maybe it was because he was worried about how to live without the bike but for some reason it had left me feeling strange. Apart from my dad he was my hero and in sme way I suppose he was a part of me. He'd been part of my growing up and part of my relationship with my dad so that was probably it. He'd looked scared and it had given me an uneasy feeling.

Dear Hugo,   BY HAND
seen you come back so I descided to write. Sory it
didnt go so good in Cherackass but they have probly
all different ways of thinking as well as the
talking. Reiser said your mother passed while you was
away so sory about that and all. What times we had
Hugo. Me, Gopf, Leo, Hansie and big Marcel in Paris
with the champeijne! We reckoned we was the kings but
it was all because what you done! Anywhey long time
ago I suppose – not a Swiss in the top 20 at the Tour
now – terrible I reckon it is!
Take care dear Hugo from Your friend old Georges You
was always prettier than me but I reckon less good
with bike pump just ask Hassenforder ! (no more
cycling for me – 40 now!)
take care my friend take care hope we see we
again soon.
10 jannuary 1961

22.01.61

Swiss Cycling
Federation,
Talstrasse 4,
8001, Zurich

Hugo Koblet
Forchstrasse 125
8125
Zollikerberg
Zurich

My dear Hugo,

I read what you said about "selling snow to eskimos", but if it's any consolation, Venezuela's loss is definitely our gain.

As I explained on the telephone, it's not a great moment. Inscriptions and revenues are down, so we've moved into a smaller office and I've let Rudi go. Thankfully Ovomaltine have renewed with the TdS, but we lost 24 races last year and Basel loses money every time it puts a meet on. Bern-Geneva will probably fold and Hartmann says GP Locle has two weeks to find a sponsor. We're in no position to take on full-time staff but you can coach the track team if you want. I will reimburse your expenses as per UCI guidleines. Just keep a log of what you spend and submit to me each month end with recepits.

I'm sorry it's not better news, but at least it's something. If we had a rider like you the finances would be much healthier!

    Affectionately yours
    Ernst Lüthi

Dear Hugo

30.01.61

RADIO BEROMÜNSTER
The voice of free Switzerland

Hugo Koblet
Forchstrasse 125
8125
Zollikerberg

Dear Mr. Hugo Koblet,

Object: Tour de Suisse bicycling event, 15-21 June 1961

In this, the year 1961, Radio Beromünster shall once more assume responsibility to enjoin the peoples of the 25 cantons with the maximum cycling activity of our confederation, to wit "The Tour de Suisse". This undertaking shall be undertaken during June and we shall transmit as is by now traditional on Medium Wave frequency 936 utilizing our technologically advanced transmission facility situated in the nether regions of Lucerne. We shall further extend our sportive commitment by disseminating (ergo disbursing electronically) the Six Days of Zurich indoor cycling race during December. Broadcasts of further popular bicycling manifestations such as the World Cycling Federation-organized World Cycling Championships and the Swiss Cycling Federation-organized Swiss Cycling Championships shall be confirmed as and when circumstances arise which shall be consistent with their confirmation.

Our expert bicycling correspondent, the estimable sports journalist Josef 'Sepp' Renggli, candidly informs us that thou art of his acquaintance and that thou art expert in all cycling matters which may be regarded as performative by nature and definition.

Mr Renggli has provided disclosure that a dialogue has occurred and that thou art disposed to contribute to the aforesaid performance-based, cycling-related broadcasts. If indeed this be the case, I do declare it a state of affairs which may be reasonably regarded as agreeable. Moreover I do confirm that such material costs as thy might incur in the implementation and execution of such shall be subject to appropriate reimbursement.

With cooperative regards,

Miss Evelyn Sammer (Secretary to Hans Jauch Esq.)
p.p. Hans Jauch Esq.

> H,   BY HAND
> THEY'RE NOT INTERESTED IN THE RADIO BECAUSE THEY
> WATCH THIS TELEVISION THING WITH GAME SHOWS AND SUCH
> LIKE. THEY DON'T CARE ABOUT A BUNCH OF OLD, FAT GUYS
> WHO RODE TEN YEARS AGO! WE'RE YESTERDAY'S NEWS!

VILLA VERA
by Freddy Stauffer
Five Star Acapulco
at your Fingertips

Hugo Koblet
Forchstrasse 125
Zollikerberg
Switzerland

Hey champ!

I called my buddy and you're on the money – there's a science guy in New York doing something called hair transplants. Goes by the name of Norman Orentreich and my pal says he's legit with the big brain and everything. Runs his studio out of Fifth Avenue (256) and my buddy says he's done the trans-panting thing for some of the big shots from Tinsel Town. His number is 516 2128341 - might even look him up myself!

Hang tight there champ – mia casa è tua casa!

KOBLET!!
you talking on the radio now nothing special say i too quiet SPEAK LOUDER KOBLET left ear 78 I am! Moresi ,Graf ,gImmi , useless lot !!! real champion ferdi the NOSE Kübler true worldchampion him!! KOBLET!! rings on his fingersandbells on his toes,, Knecht that was not Ferdinand Kbler! IRON HANS pull a train he could,, great bull neck on him he had light on your feet I recken you KOBLET!
   Bertrand Blattmann half-blind!! raced with Suter I did double/crossed me he Suter-swine we called him why you say?? jokes a joke took it too far is my say so KOBLET!. Notter the bastardpromised the father promise is a promise I say, been round there I did out cold he was old CH0ppy learned him7 cheer up speak louder mumbling KOBLET !!

   CHOPard.

Dear Hugo

Swiss Cycling
Federation,
Schaffhauserstrasse
272, 8057, Zurich

Hugo,

There's a room here you can have for a few weeks if needs be. We've been using it for storage since we moved in but we can empty it quite easily. There's space for a bed and a small wardrobe, and a there's a sink you can wash in. You'll have to shower a-at the track, but it's only a five minute walk and it's only temporary.

Ernst

```
H,                                                    BY HAND
I called home a couple of times but no reply pal.
I guess you're busy with events and parties and what
have you but anyway hope everything's ok? I was
speaking to Sepp and he said he really enjoys working
with you on the radio! Heard you're putting a few kilos
on that's normal if you're not getting out on the bike
no offense or anything like that just a joke between
two old mates is all pal. I was wondering if you
fancied coming out for a ride some time! At our age we
need think about staying in shape! Call if you like
buddy and you find a minute! (my number, in case you
lost it: 44 32 91 )
F
```

02.04.62

Enrico Mattei
Via Sebastopoli 88,
20196, Milano

Mr H Koblet
C/O Swiss Cycling
Schaffhauserstrasse
272
8057
Zurich

Dear Hugo,

I have spoken to my Swiss colleagues about the proposed petrol station at Oerlikon. I don't think there will be any further issues. They shared their concerns, but I reiterated my personal commitment to the project and invited them to expedite matters. I confirmed that the petrol station should be branded "Hugo Koblet", and they acquiesced. My understanding is that with a fair wind me we may look forward to a grand opening – and you to a new start - in June.

Yours sincerely,
Enrico Mattei

Federal Tax Administration

Fiscal Services; Debt Management
mbpa/pac/88751-1962   rwq9012600001236   212 517 des: RWQ876

Communication no: 01288641230
Case Code: 64892008961-6

                                                    KOBLET HUGO
                                             FORCHSTRASSE 125
                                                            8125
                                                    ZOLLIKERBERG

Dear Sir/Madam,

Each year the Federal Tax Administration performs rigorous checks to fiscal declarations, in order to verify that the information furnished is precise. We wish to inform you that, according to our records, your earnings declarations for the year:
1952
1953
1956
1957
1958
We present the errors evidenced on the subsequent pages.
If you are in agreement with our findings, you may regularize your fiscal position by forwarding the sum of CHF140,723.76 within 30 days of receipt of this communication. In this case, the interest charge imposed for late remittance shall be reduced by 33 per cent. To affect payment, you may submit a bank draft or cashier's cheque made payable to the Federal Tax Administration, along with the enclosed remittance form. The form specifies the total amount due, including the reduced sanction.
If, on the other hand, you believe our finding to be incorrect, please provide written supporting evidence within 30 days. Alternatively, you may present yourself in person at the debt management section of our offices at KAPELLENWEG 54. In this case, please provide such documentation as you believe to be pertinent to your declaration, in order that our administrators may execute further checks to verify your fiscal position.
We invite you to respond within 30 days. No further notice will be provided.

CENTRAL DIRECTOR
Uli Kaltz
LM NT RW TX RR RS
Communication created 12/05/1962

Dear Hugo

HUGO KOBLET
PIRELLI

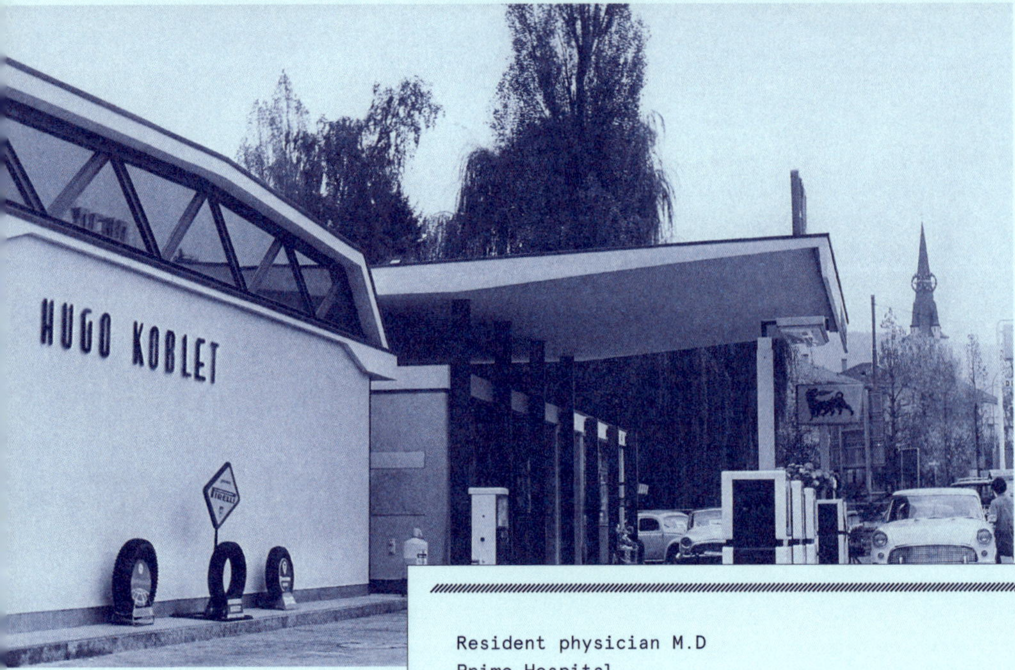

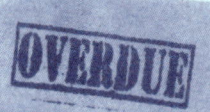

Resident physician M.D
Prime Hospital
License # 345524

PATIENT: Koblet Hugo
Forchstrasse 125
8125
Zollikeberg

PRESCRIPTION: Valium 5mg tablets 4x daily

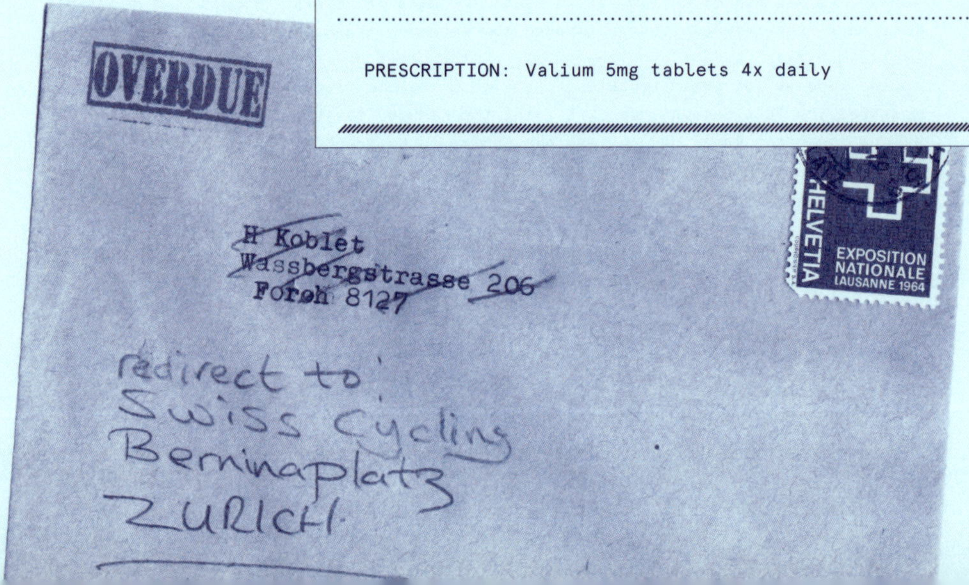

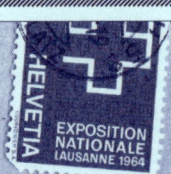

OVERDUE
H Koblet
Wassbergstrasse 206
Forch 8127
HELVETIA
EXPOSITION
NATIONALE
LAUSANNE 1964
redirect to:
Swiss Cycling
Berninaplatz
ZURICH

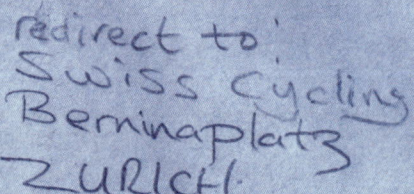

I'm at home in Schaffhausen, in case you happened to be wondering. I won't be coming back, and I won't forgive you. Father won't be paying the rent, and he certainly won't be propping up Rolf's latest useless restaurant. If you choose to stay in the house it's up to you, but I'm not sure you'd want it all on the front page of the paper. It's up to you.

Two weeks Hugo. Two weeks.

8th July 2021

Zurich isn't a big place and I knew lots of people from the cycling communitie. I'd heard rumours that he had money troubles and I knew they'd closed one of his petrol stations because we'd driven past a couple of times.
It was all boarded up and there was nobody there. The big one at Oerlikon wa still going and I used to pass it often. The problem was it gave me an uneasy feeling so I avoided looking at it just in case and I never went there for fuel. I told myself it was because there were lots of petrol station in that part of Zurich and I suppose that was true at least. There was one just round the corner on Schwamen-dingenstrasse so I would go there instead. I told myself it was just a coincidense that I never went to the Hugo Koblet one but it wasn't. It was the opposite of a coincidense but we all lie to ourself sometimes don't we? That's the way we make tthings which shouldn't be normal seem normal.

10th July 2021

Sometimes I write badly and make mistakes with the typing . It's because I can't type as quickly as my brain thinks and I worry I will forget thoughts. So I type fast to try to keep up with the thoughts but that seems to make it worse because the fatsrer I type the more the memories seem to come.Sometimes it's not eeasy so sorry for that and I'll try to explain better:-

   I was trying to convince myself that I'd moved on with my life and in most respects I had moved on. I was very happy with Elke, and we loved each other. Wwith every day which passed I was surer and surer that she was the one for me so it was really just a aquestion of time before I asked her and I'd already started putting money aside. Then my mum was fine and mr K had made it clear what he intended to do. He said he wanted to do a few more years and then for me to take over the business. (if everything was in order of course.).

   I suppose you could say that he and my mum had become a couple - but goodness it had been slow going! At the beginning they hadn't known what to say or how to be with each other and that was because of their ages and the circcumstanses. When me and my sister were there they always became quite serious and formal. She said 'you're so prim and starchy mother' but it was understandable so

I told her not to be hard on them and to give them time. After all not everyone is the same and we didn't know what it was like to be in their shoes.

    Mr K never talked to me about mum while we were at work, but one Saturday morning he askd what I thought about calling him Hans. (That was his name you see?) The problem was that it didn't seem natural to either of us after all those years. After a couple of hours he said 'that was a bloody silly idea wasn't it?' and we went back to normal. He offered me one of his mints and we set off to clear a place at Hottingen. It was funny that. Later on when he and mum properly lived together I'd call him 'Hans' from time to time. I'd say"Now then Hans, I hope you're treating my mother correctly!!'. It was only a kjoke though.

10th July 2021
(evening)

WHAT Happened was that one afternoon I was picking some furniture up from a care home in Zollikon. We had to wait and there was a documentry news thing on the television. The Tour dde Suisse was on andthey were asking everyone why the Swis riders always lost and the Italiand were much better.. At a point they interviewed Hugo about the good old days and lots of people gathered round BECAUSE IT WAS HIM.

    The questions the guy was asking him were stupid. That annoyed me but I could tell straight away that something was wronf. I knew him you see so I could tell just by looking at him that something was broken. It made me think of that last night at the Hallenstadion when he'd been speaking about about what he was going t do with his life. He'd been pretending that everything was going to alright then and he was pretending that everything was alright now!. He was pretending to be the Hugo Koblet that everyone wanted him to be if you see what I mean?

    What I think is thyat people expected him to behave in a certain way and because he'd been doing it for so long he didn't know any other way.

11th July 2021

I didn't finish about the Tour de Suisse interview. What really got me was that that they were all grinning but nothing was real and everything was super-fiscial. It wasn't a real conversation because it was like a script

Dear Hugo

tthat they had to read out without thinking. It was all just because it was being on tele vision and it was done for people who just sat there on their divans and didn't want to think about anything serriously. They didn't care about Hugo Koblet as a human being so they just repeated the same old stupid rubbish. It was as if his job was to remind people of the times he and Ferdi had been winning. He just had to re-arrange the same old words because that's what made them feel good. They'd call him 'the blonde falcon', Hugo the beautiful, 'the pedaller of charm" or whatever, even though it was 1963 &and the person they were talking to wasn't any of those things. He was a middel-aged man who weighed 100 kilograms but he would smile and go along with it politely because that was they wanted to hear. I think he wqas in a sort of trap and he had to keep reliving what he'd once been. His whole life was a performance and that stopped him from moving forward and being something else. He didn't know how to say no because he always tried to please everyone else and he was supposed to be the superman Hugo Koblet. He couldn't ever admit to being unhappy or even just normal. H e couldn't go back to being the normal Hugo Koblet from Aussersihl because he was like an actor and he only had one role which he couldnt get out of it. He had to play Hugo Koblet the great tour de Farnce winner so that's what he did. It seemed that the 22 years old cyclist I'd run alongside when I was a boy had become the unhappiest person be in the world and nobody had nozticed or they chose not to care. They just carried on and so he did as well. It upset me.

....

13th July 2021

I Forgot to mention that I often think about how it happened the way it did. Itr try to imagine all the Six Day races with the sleepless nights and the pills and whatever they would have taken to keep going like that. I think about him trevelling through the night with Armin Van Büren, going all over to ride the track. All those madisons – one day inGermany then France, over in Belgiium,Holland, Italy and everywhere. Being friends with people like Coppi, winning the Giro and the Tour like that, all those parties and probably (if its true what they said) all those women. Then whatever it was that happened at the 1952 Tour de Suisse and the 1953 Giro with Coppi , those terrible moments at the Tour in 1953 and 1954. The K&K situation in a small country like ours. I mean hee was still a young man then and he didn't know how to manage money or fame or any of those things – he had no idea! People assumed it was all easy and I suppose it was. After all, things are always easy until they aren't anymore!! Then the glamourous wife, all the money and the jets-set lifestyle, not having a dad and the situation with the mother. Culumbia, Venezuela, Mexico... what I mean is that sort of thing is going to be exsausting. It's going to change a person whether he like it or not, and you can't just change back. You can't just decide to be the person you once were or the person you want to be. You can't be Hugo Koblet one minuate and a normal person the next.

    This probably doesn't make much sense but it was what I was thinking after that interview and it's what I still think today.

....

14th July 2021

This PROBABLY SEEMS STUpid but I remembered something after I finished last night. that's always the way isn't it ? It was nearly midnight so I couldn't very well start again even though I was tempted so I wrote it down and put it on the bedside table in case I forgot again and it's this:-

    It was one morning and I was having a conversation with mr K ABOUT IT. I Was trying to explain and he said something which I never forgot. What he said was that it would have been best if Hugo had come out on a few staurday mornings with us. He said he would be able to suck mints and listen to terrible music on the the radio like we did because we always tried to find the worst songs and to give them marks out of 10 for hopelesness). It was a really good idea by mr K because if he could just come and move furniture with us for a couple of hours we could decide to talk about anything which wasn't cycling. That would have been hard for me but I know that we would have managed becaue mr K was clever like that and he would have seen to it.

    Mr K said 'I could tell him about the beermat collection!' Now I immagine that would seem absurd but I know for a fcat that it wouldn't have been. Mr K had beermats from all over the world and he had friends he used to swap them

Dear Hugo

with. He knew everything about where the beermats
came from and the customs of the local people. He even
knew about the rivers the water in the beer came from!
He seemed to know everything about everywhere and he
became animated when he got talking about Australia,
Russia or Kenya or wherever. Hugo would have liked it
because he was always one for travelling and adventure.
Obviously we wouldn't only have talked about the beermats
but i was sure that if only he didn't have to pretend to be
Hugo Koblet it would have helped and he would have had
something to look forward to on a Saturday morning.
I know you can't unmake yourself or something like that
but with us maybe it would have been better.

15th July 2021

When Elke's dad told me he Koblet had split up with his
wife I just shrugged and said it was a shame but he wa
responsible for his life like everyone else!. We had the
wedding planning to be getting on with and we would drive
around on Sundays (n not only in Zurich) trying to decide
where we wanted to live. We had to find the right house in
the right area becau-se we were planning on starting
a family as quickly as we could.

16th July 2021

I always read what I wrote before I syart again and I just
read that from yesterday when I had to stop. What I was
starting to say is that I got on with my life and tried to
ignore it. That was my mistake and that'swhat I mean
about getting things straight in. The problem is that
sometimes there are so many things going on that you can't
get them all straight because you don't have enough time
to think everything through as you should. You just keep
going because you think you don't have the answer and
that's how things start to build up. You finish up with all
these useless problems one on top of the other and if youre
not careful they all get bigger and become a big confusion
which overpowers you. You can't get rid of it and it starts
to change the way you think abd behave. What I'm trying to
say is that my reaction was wrong eve butI was young and I
hadn't learned to think things through and find solusions..
So each time I read about Hugo or heard him speak on the
radio this bad feeling would come over me. It was like a

black cloud or a sort of guiltiness inside me which
I couldn't understand. That was why I told myself it had
nothing to do with me and tried to ignore it and ignore him.
I was wishing that it would go away even though I don't
know how that would have happened.. The last thing I want
to say is that from time to time I'd be somewhere (it could
be anywhere) and this feeling I couldn't identifY would
happen to me. When I stopped and asked myself why it was
happening I always thought of Hugo and my dad so I tried
to push it away and get on wuith things. So it wasn't that I
wasn't bothered. I pretended I wasn't because in fact it was
the opposite. I was bothered too much. The pain it gave me
was probably or possibly to do with that first afternoon at
Zillis and my dad. Cycling had been one of the main things
of our relation-ship and even towards the end when things
had been hard it had never let us down. We didnt always
agree but when we talked about it we forgot whatever other
troubles we had. So subconsciesly it perhaps reminded
me of dad's illness and of what I'd lost. I probably haven't
exèplained that very well but but it was a confuse ion and it
took me a long time to understand it all.

Hugo Koblet
Radio Station
Lausanne

Dear mr Hugo Koblet,

My name is Otto Bieri and I am of Rheinfelden . I am sorry for the disturbance but I hope You might remember Me because We met at the Tour de Suisse way back in 1953 but probably You will not .

To remind You of 1953 my Wife who is called Greta had birthed twin boys and We had named them with Hugo and Ferdinand . We brung them to the time trial and it was the first time We had been out together in a Family way so We seemed to make quite a specticle with lots of Persons wanting to see them and know the story . You might remember that We have all made an interview together for the Radio and there was a photograf in the Sports Newspaper .

This it was a very special day for Me and my Greta and often people they talk to us about it still so I can say Hugo and Ferdi are a little bit known here in Rheinfelden and all because I was a great admirer of you and your Cycling accomplischments .

Hugo likes the cycling very much and He has understud everything about who You are and why his name is Hugo . The Brothers they will be celebrating their ten years on april 30 so We will be making a special Party with their Friends here in our modest House in Rheinfelden .

Dear mr Koblet if it might be possible for You could come to Rheinfelden and re-meet with us it would be a magic for me and my Greta and also for Hugo and the brother Ferdi . We can arrange everything and there is a very nice Hotel Garni here which is very cumferting and has all the modern accutriments for hair-drying, in-the-bed boozing , TV watching , Radio , Food , Telephone talking , clothes ironing and laundering ones personage . Or You can stay with Us at Our House which would be a wonderful honour even if You probably would not want it as We are of modest faculty and not of high culture at all .

If You are not able I perfectly understand . We are simple people after all and not at all of high culture. I thank You anyhow and send warm salutations from me, my wife Greta and our boys Hugo & Ferdi who met you in 1953 here in Rheinfelden.

From Otto Bieri, Denschiweg 12, Rheinfelden 79618

IN THE SUPERIOR COURT
FOR THE CANTON OF ZURICH

Order ref: 1783/ZCH62

SONJA KOBLET (NÉE BÜHL) b. 8/4/1933, Schaffhausen
Petitioner,

vs.

HUGO KOBLET b. 21/3/1925, Zurich
Respondent.

This: 3/11/1962

Marriage Date: 6/12/1954
Parish: Fraumünster
Ref: FR8512CD54

JUDGMENT AND DECREE FOR LEGAL SEPARATION
WITHOUT CHILDREN

IT IS HEREBY ORDERED, ADJUDGED AND DECREED as follows:

1. A decree of legal separation is entered on the grounds of infidelity and mental cruelty on behalf of the respondent. The couple shall remain married for a period of 24 months (or until such time as a material reconciliation is achieved), whereupon the marriage shall be declared void.

2. The couple have no children or other dependents.

3. The parties' property and debt should be divided as set forth in the Findings of Fact and Conclusions of Law.

SUPERIOR COURT JUDGE

Mr. Hugo Koblet
90 Dörflistrasse,
8050
Zuürich

Dear mr Hugo Koblet!,

I am again Otto Bieri of Rheinfelden ! You have given Me and my Greta a gigantic news and We have not the words to thank You ! The party for Hugo &Ferdi will be placed here at our House with 17.00. Our idea is for You to make a special entrance at 17.30 though of course You may also arrive before if it pleases You to spend some time with our humble family .

    I have for you made the Prenotation at HOTEL GARNI which is on Werderstrasse but if You prefer We can make another arrangement or You may wish to stay with Us here in our House . This would be a magical happening for Us and my Greta I must say she keeps the House very ti nicely even though we are of modest cap- erbilities and not at all shick. Wonderful wonderful WONDERFUL mr Koblet our little Hugo will be thrilling . Thank You again from the BOTTOMS OF OUR HEARTS and We see You with We here on 30 april.

From Otto & Great Bieri, Denschiweg 12, Rheinfelden 79618

15.07.64

Switzerland
H.Q., Rue de
Lutry, Lausanne
Hugo Koblet
Station 90
Dörflistrasse,
8050 Zürich

Dear Mr Koblet,

Despite our previous correspondence and your personal assurances, I'm sad to note that we still haven't received remittance for our invoice dated 3 January. I remind you that our terms remain 60 days net, and as such the invoices for February, March and April are also now overdue.
In total over 200,000 litres remain outstanding, and this is no longer sustainable. Please contact me immediately, in order that we can establish a recovery plan. If I don't hear from you I shall have no alternative but to issue court proceedings, and to suspend deliveries pending a reassignment of the lease.

Yours sincerely,

Erich Forst
Financial Controller

Dear Hugo

```
20.07.64
La Gazzetta dei
Sportivi
Via Galileo Galilei
7, Milan
Milan

Hugo Koblet
90 Dörflistrasse,
8050
Zürich
```

Dear Koblet,

It was a shame you weren't with us at the Giro. It was a great pleasure to welcome the other former winners, and your absence was most unfortunate.

    Your interview reminded me of my conversation with Clerici. He said he'd achieved more than he could have imagined, while you perceive your career has having been "a failure". You assert that you were an "inferior" rider because you never won the World Championship or the Hour Record, and that saddens me greatly.

    Objectively you were a champion. Moreover it's a matter of fact that neither Bartali nor Magni wore the rainbow jersey, whilst average riders like Muller (and the "champion" Beheyt) did. Nor did Bobet or Bartali accomplish the hour, but the notion that they weren't champions is patently absurd. Whilst there's no doubt you could have broken the Hour Record, you honoured your sport and gave pleasure to millions. Of course success in sports is often relative, but you should be proud of your accomplishments.

    Good luck with your new venture. Rest assured that you are welcome at our races whenever your calendar permits.
Vincenzo Togliani

```
Louison,
Christiane, Philippe
and Maryse Bobet,
Rue Fontan 22,
Saint-Brieuc.
```

My dear friend Hugo,

Long time no hear! Christiane and I will be in Davos 2-9 December. We will have the children, and it would be nice if you and Sonja could join us. I told Philippe you are better descending on skis than on the bike!

Kind regards,
Louison!

IN THE SUPERIOR COURT
FOR THE CANTON OF ZURICH

Order ref: 1783/ZCH62

SONJA KOBLET (NÉE BÜHL) b. 8/4/1933, Schaffhausen
Petitioner,

vs.

HUGO KOBLET b. 21/3/1925, Zurich
Respondent.

This: 29/10/1964

Marriage Date: 6/12/1954
Parish: Fraumünster
Ref: FR8512CD54

> H,
> I've called 3 times but you've always out! I can't pay you if you don't send me a bill!
> Jonny

JUDGMENT AND DECREE FOR DIVORCE

IT IS HEREBY ORDERED, ADJUDGED AND DECREED as follows:

2. A decree of divorce is entered on the grounds of infidelity and mental cruelty on behalf of the respondent. Absent further intervention, the decree shall be issued 3/12/1964, whereupon the marriage shall be declared void.

2. The couple have no children or other dependents.

4. The parties' property and debt should be divided as set forth in the Findings of Fact and Conclusions of Law.

SUPERIOR COURT JUDGE

OVERDUE

URGENT

HUGO KOBLET
Dörflistrasse 90
Zurich 8050

URGENT

HUGO KOBLET
Dörflistrasse 90
Zurich 8050

18th July 2021

It was a Monday afternoon - 2 nd December. I was with Martin and we were on the way back from Baden because we'd been clearing a townhouse on the river bank. The owner had been an important barrister and his son and daughter were there. It was obvious they didn't like each other and he seemed drunk. She was quite unk rude to Martin. I told Martin not to let it worry him because some people can handle grief and others not. The most important thing was to be polite and serious in our work. I told him it was a dificcult moment for them and he should n't take it personally.

    Martin was a good boy. He worked hard and I liked him. I suppose that was because he was the same age as I had been when I started there and I liked having the responsability of teaching him. w

    The sun was shinig and there was a beautiful clear sky. I think there were still leaves on the trees but it's possible that thre weren't. Maybe I immagined that once upon a time and now I've convinced myself that it's true. I know that can happen because I've learned that everyone creates their own story and I don't see why I would be any different.

    Wwe finished quite early and I think it would have been the 15.00 news bulletin because the sun was starting to set. They were asking people about all the foreign workers coming into Switzerland and there was something about the Pope being in India. I wasn't really paying attention to it because Martin and I were talking but then I caught the radio newsman saying "Hugo Koblet". I told Martin to stop talking and the newsman said there had been an accident. It had happened in the morning on the road between Esslingen and Mönchaltorf, to the south of ZUrich. He said that there weren't other cars involved and that Hugo had been taken to hospital in Uster. Martin said "that will be near the Kreuzgaragage where we sometimes go for diesel!" What I said to Martin wasn't very nice and I shouldn't have done it. It wasn't his fault because he was only 16 or so and he didn''t understand who Koblet was. I apologized afterwards and he said it wasn't anything and he was sorry as well. I liked that about Martin becuae he meant it : - he didn't just say it because the thought he was supposed to. He was young but he was from a good family and that was mr K had taken him. i

Dear Hugo

I dropped Martin off at the station and went to the telephone cabin even though I had that terrible feeling in my stomach again. I told Elke I was going straight to Uster and she said we would go too in that case and her dad would take her. She said she'd ring my mum and told me to drive carefully and not do anything stupid.

We couldn't get into the car park because it's a small hospital and there were hundreds of people there. I parked on the roadside about 200 metres away and I remember walking towards the hospital because it felt all wrong- somehow it felt like it was 04.00 on the morning even if it was about 17.00 on the afternoon. When I walked through the gates it seemed everyone from cycling was there. I saw lots of people I knew and that made it worse instead of better. Van Büren, Clerici and Metzger talking to journalists. When Koblet's wife came out of the hospital everyone stopped talking and looked at the floor. That was when I knew it must have been very serious. Elke's dad was talking to some other people who were about his age. They all had their hands in their pockets and one of them was shaking his head. Leo Amberg was there and I shook his hand as I passed because I could tell he recognized me even if there were no words to say and he looked terrible.

Elke she was stood on her own and she was shivering a bit because the sun had gone in and it had turned cold. We hugged and we didn'z normally do that in public places. She said she'd told my mum and promised we'd go even if it was just a for a few minutes on the way home. She said Hugo had crashed into a pear tree and they were operating and that was all she knew. After a while someone came out and explained that he was bad but they were hopeful. The journalists were quite respectfull but it was hard to hear. He said he couldn't say anything else and it was best that everyone went home.

I went in the van with Elke and we passed where the acacident must have happened. There bwas a tree close to the side of the road and a few people were stood around it. Elke always says the thing she remembers most is that when my mum asked me if I was hungry I didn't answer and she had to ask me again. She says that after that I didn't speak any more, except to say goodnight.

19th July 2021

I didn't sleep well and it was before dawn when I walked to get the newspaper. It was on the front page, and there was a photo of the tree with his car against it which I thought was a terrible thing to publish. Blick was suggesting he'd been trying to take his own life because he hadn't braked and there were no skid-.marks or anything like that. Some of the reports said he must have had a seizure or fallen asleep and there were people refusing to believe the idea that he had done it on purpose. I think the idea was probably too terrible so tyhey convinced themselves uit wasn't true and it couldn't happen. That's understandable after-all because he was a public person and they probably had a s sense of guilt as I did. I felt responseable because in some way I was resposeable. He was the Hugo Koblet that cycling had created and without it he would have had a different life andhe wouldn't done what he'd done.

There were lots of rumours. People were saying he'd been seen getting into his car in Forch a few minutes before the crash. That was where his wife was living and it was close to where the accident
happened. The thing is that Esslingen was to the south of Forch and Zurich was to the north. It was a very quiet country road and it was in the opposite direction. If he was going home he would nevr have gone that way and he didn't have any business there so there bwas no reason that anyone could think for him to have been there. Elke said it was a strange way to do if he wanted try to kill yourself because it was n't intelligent or logical. She sdaid there was a high probability it wouldn't work and she was right. The problem was that if you are in such a bad state that you want to kill yourself you're not thinking clearly or using logic. If you're trying to kill yourself in a car it's because nothing is working anymore and everything is broken.

Someone said he'd been seen driving up and down past that pear tree 3 or4 times.

20th July 2021

On Wednesday I got up very early . I was usually up at 6 but it hink it was 04.30 or something because I had to wait before I went to get the newspapers because the kiosk wasn't opewn yet. I went to the kiosk and waited a few minutes because I wanted to read everything before Elke woke and we ate breakfast. In the one of them (I think

Dear Hugo

Neue Zürcher Nachrichten) there was a interview with the surgeon. He said Hugo had been in and out of conscieous and that was a good sign. He said it was still a critical situation but he was optimitic they could save him.

When I told Elke she said, "That's good news " but as far as I was concerned it wasn't. I explained to her that I didn't want them to save him because if he wanted to be saved he wouldn't have tried to stop his life and he wouldn't be in that Hospital. Elke said it was wrong to think like that and it was a sin to try to take your own life. I said she was wrong and it was nothing to with God. I told her he didn't have anyone so it didn't make any difference. She said it was best if I just went to work because I was saying nonsense and I was nervous. I said she didn't undersatand anything because she didn't listen and she wasn't intelligent enough. I said he was Hugo Koblet and he deserved to die with at least some dignity while he was sleeping. I told his life should finish peacefully and without pain while he was dreaming of the day he met Sugar Ray-Robinson at the Tour or beating Coppi at the Gran- Prix Des Nations or riding into Rome in theepink jersey. I said whatever life they thought to be saving would have been terrible because otherwise he wouldn't have done what he'd done. Anyway everything was ruined and his body was ruined and that's what i told Elke. I said Ididn't want that for him and I knew my dad wouldn't have wanted it and neither would her dad but he wouldn't have had the courage to say it.When she asked what I meant I said it was because yuo weren't supposed to say it and he was one of those people who just went along with the rules. I shouldn't have said that because it was unkind and I felt bad all day. I apologized when I got home that that evening and told her I I hadn't meant what I'd said. Elke laughed and said she knew I hadn't. She told me her big mistakwe was that she'd married an idiot. She made two fists like a boxer and ssaid "Do that again mister and I'll give you Sugar Ray Robinson!". (She didn't mean it obviously.)

....

22nd July 2021

I was sad when he died but I was pleased that it was over. Even Elke agreed that it was better that way because he hadn't been getting better at all.He'd been in a coma for two days and everything that a human being could break was broken. His brain was damaged and he wouldnt have walked again. I like to think that his dreams were good and that he went without agonies. I wanted for him to go up there and ride an omnium at the Vel d'Hiv or the Vigorelli with Coppi and Ockers. That was what I wanted and I wanted for me and my dad to be there watching.

We all went to the funeral, even my sister. It was at the Fraumünster Church, where he'd been married almost 10 years ago to the day. That made me nostaljic because I'd been there that day (well, outside the church anyway) and I wondered how things would have been for him if he and his wife had managaed to make a normal life with ordinary jobs and children . That was probably because Elke had told that she was expecting the day before and it was what everything we'd been hoping for.

We were there at least an hour early but we didn't get anywhere near the church.OF Of course there were people there from cycling but there were politicians ,actors and other sportsmen as ewll. They had speakers outside so we could hear and I remember standing on tip-toes to see Kübler and Bobet.

....

23rd July 2021

We called the boy Hugo in case you were wondering. He was the reason we'd met after all, and Elke knew her dad would approve of it. Mum was thrilled because Besides dad would have loved it, and he'd have loved Hugo.

Mr K DIDN'T KNOW HOW TO be a grandftaher at first. He was all fingers and thumbs but once he got used to it he and Hugo became best friends. You couldn't separate them!. Hugo rode until he was 18 or so but then he went and did military service and stopped. He started again when he was in his 30s, abou tthe time Camenzind won the World Championship. He works for UBS and his boy, Mathias, is a very good rider as well. He has a beautiful carbon bike with 12 gears and he says it's under 7 kilos!

His sisters are called Anna and Clara, by the way. Anna was born in 1967 and she works at the town hall. Her husband is involved in softwear and they have two boys both at university. The younger one is called Robert and he's the cyclist. I've been promising him I'd write all this down for a few years so I'm pleased it's finished because at least it won't get lost.

Dear Hugo

Clara is my other daughter and she' a maths teacher. ShE always has her head in a book. She's always off at some rally or other but she doesn't have a car and now she says she won't fly. She cycles everywher and she has one of those car-go-bikes for the shopping. She won't eat meat or cheese and she says she doesn't miss it. She gives me worry nbut has her group of friednds and she says she's not interested in being with a man. She was born in 1969 and then Elke said that was enough. My wife she pas

25th July 2021

Elke died two years ago and i haven't really spoken about it. I'm still shufling around in this world but without her I feel as if I'm not really part of it. I try to be enthuesiastic when the family is here but most of the days are the same. I get up and do things, but mainly I just wait for the day to end. I feel like the fight has gone out of me. I loved her so much, you see?.

28th July 2021

I finally want to say that writing this out has been very good for me. I think Elke would be pleased because sher told me I had to go on with my life and not just wait for it to finish. I admit its no been difficult,, and sometimes I just sit because I don't know what to do. She wouldn't like that and the worst thing is that sometimes I've felt like ive been letting her down. These past weeks have been diffrrent though. Remembering everything has given the days meaning and ive woken up with a sense of purpose and enthusiasm.

 Anyway I cant say we weren't happy beca-use we were. Mr K started working 4 days-a-week and then 3 and that was how we did it. I took over the business completely in October 1971 but I'd been running it for a few years anyway by then so that was that. I wouldn't say I missed seeing him (because you see we were still together a lot at mums) But I missed our Saturday mornings and work wasn't so much fun without him. I hadn't really thought anbout it before but suddenly I was the responsable and there were eight other people relying on me and the the descisions I made. We got more staff and

 more vehicles and started working for the town hall as well as private people. We were succesfull I suppose you might say, and of course that was good for me and Elke.

The only thing is that I felt a little bit lonely sometimes. I got on well with everyone and I ttried to look after theem all. People tended to stay with us and I know we had a good reputation. The only problem with being the boss was that sometimes I just felt a little bit isolated if you see what I mean. Looking back, i think that was probably one of the reasons I started up with the Saturday mornings.. It wasn't every week because I could never have done that with 3 kids. It was more like once a month or so just to feellike I was doing some real work and not organizing other people to do everything. I suppose i Just felt a little bit gilty because for me work was something you did with your body and not your brain. I usually asked Martin because I liked spending time with him and he was a good hand. He was serious and he had a girl, Sara. They were saving as best they could for flat so I WAS HELPING HIM AND THAT WAS Helping me.

Anyway it was in 1974. A guy who was a restaurantur had died, and we had to go and empty his place. They'd said it was just a few personal things, so maybe 2 or 3 hours. That was why I said we would sdo in on the Saturday yousee, so as we could be home for lunch. Martin was tall and narrow but he ate like a dragon and he always flattered Elke about her cooking. So she looked forward to having him for lunch and so did the kids .

The way it worked was that we just picked up whatever was there and deposited it it. Obvioulsy if it was junk we threw it away but anything of any money value we took to the unit because it had to go to auction. Often these people had no family and sometimes they had troubles you see? Sometimes we had to throw away photogra -phs, passports and letters, but we were the last ones and after a while you didn't think anything of it. That's strange because it was of someones life but I guess it was just a job like any other. You didn't really think about the person anymore4 and I admit that staurdays were always a bit like that. We were working, but we we were also there to enjoying ourselves. That probably isn't right but it's the truth.

The best part was the journey with the mints and the radio, talking about the lunch we knew Elke would be makingfor us.

Dear Hugo

Sometimes there would be someone the- re from the family but usually there wasn't. If there had been family they probably wouldn't have neded us to take everything away you see? Besides I tried to make sure there was no family for the Saturday jobs. I don't want you to think we didn't do it for serious because we did. It was just a bit less serious and a bit less formal. It was mainly a way to spend time together and FORGet about work, which I suppose might seema bit odd. I suppose it's what Clara would call a parradox.

I don't want to go into too much detail because it wouldn't be right. I do want t to say that Martin didn't know anything about it so there is no way any blame can be placed with him. The truthis that I saw the name of the deceased on some letters and there was a normal family photograph in a picture frame on a sideboard. I knew straight away who it was that had died and I can't deny that. Martin might have k known as well but he didn't say any thing and as far as I know he never knew what was in the box.

It was an old cardboard box and it was 50 cm x 30 cm, something like that. It was quite dusty and the tape holding it together had dried up and come loose. The re was a big letter H on it which had been written with a green crayon or something. It was already faded but I admit that when I saw it my heart skipped and I struggled to breath for a while . I only glanced inside it for a couple of seconds because I already knew what it was. I didn't say anything to Martin but that was normal.

I want to say as well that we did the work in the same wway that we always did. We acted quite correctly so there was nothing that happened in that place that wasn't right. The mistake I made was a mistake when we came to the unloading.

For a reason which was totally delibrate I left one of the boxes in the van and didn't give it to Martin. I could easily say that I forgot to unload it but that would be a lie. I I'd had 2 hours to think about what I was going to do with it. Ii stole a box which wasn't mine and whichever way you think about it that was a theft and I am a criminal. There is no other way to decscribe it and no other way to interpret it.

29th July 2021

So that's the story for better or for worse. I don't suppose it will matter to anyone because it was a long time ago and there's almost nobody left who can remember Koblet now. A few might say:- "oh yes! the peddlar du charme!" and they might say something silly about the comb. but that's all and there isn't a monument or a museum or anything. We Swiss are a bit funny like that. What I mean is that if he had been in French or ITAlianor Belgian there would be lots of information. They would be statues and streets named after him but here there is almost nothing. There's Hugo Koblet Strasse but the sign doesn't even mention the Tour de France and the city doesn't do anything . Maybe it's because Küübler went on until he was 99 and the older he became the more the legend of Ferdi the nose seemed to grow.. The idea of Ferdi the patriot got bigger and bigger and the memory of Hugo grew smaller and smaller. I,m not an important person but I want to say that I consider myself a lucky one. I was lucky to meet Hugo Koblet that afternoon in Zillis and lucky with everything that happened aas a consaequence. What I mean is that when I was a boy my dad took me to a bike race and I ran along a mountain-top with Hugo Koblet. Who else can say a magic like that? That was the start of my cycling life you see? When I was a young man I met my wife because of Hugo (and of course my dad) and because of Elke I became a father and we made a good life together. So even if neither of us knew it, when Koblet smiled at me as I ran alongside him, it lasted a lifetime. If you think about it, that's a sort of miracle. The bike has been such a big part of my life that I often wonder what I would done without it. I wonder how people who don't have it manage to live their lives!. How can you say you've lived if you haven't experienced going fast on a sports bike? How can you say you've lived if you haven't ridden to the top of a great Alpine pass on a warm summer afternoon? (I stopped riding my bike 10-years ago because the children asked me to). I want to say that was a mistake and I wont ever get used to it. They won't like it but I should have said "no!" because without it everything is more complicate d and I'm not as happy. I've regretted it ever since but a promise is a promise even if it's a stupid one. There isn't a day when I don't think about cycling, or dream about being on my bike again. I can only watch the races on the tv now but from time to time I can picture

Dear Hugo

myself on the red Cilo in my dreams or out on the tandem with my Elke. Sometimes I wake up quite happy and I know it's because I've had one of theose dreams. About Hugo, I just want to say 2 things. The first one is that he was too good for this world ,or this world wasn't good enough for him. It didn't deserve a person like him and I think that was why he couldn't be in it any more.. I think it broke him and when I think about bthat it saddens me quite much. He should have been more selfish and probably he should have cheated like the others. But he didn't know how to do that. I have reed a lot of books and things about him and everyone say he was always kind and always 100percent correct. Even when he was near the end he was smilinmg and trying to be kind with the others. Nobody ever says anything bad about him and how can they? There is nothing bad you can say about Hugo Koblet as a cyclist and nothing bad you can say about him as a man. THe other thing is about one of the letters. It's the one from the Giro organizer at the end of his life when he was talking like it was all finished and he hadn't been a good rider because he hadt won the World Championshsip or broken the Hour like Coppi and Anquetil. When I read that it broke my heart. Not the part aout the hour record because that doesn't matter at all. It was right that he only won one Tour and one Giro because if miracles happened over and over again tbhey wouldn't be miracles. What I mean is that if there had been somebody to help him like children or a normal family for him to love, he might not have died. I don't mean I'm not glad that he died when he did because the injuries were terrible and he didn't deserve to suffer otr to feel alone. I JUST think it's sad that it happened so badly, and I think it's shameful that certain people denied the truth about the suicide part. I hope that makes sense but probably it does't so I'm sorry. Anyway I suppose

....

30th July 2021   Well I suppo